Self-Instructor in the Art of Hair Work

by Mark Campbell

SELF-INSTRUCTOR

IN THE

ART OF HAIR WORK,

DRESSING HAIR,

MAKING CURLS, SWITCHES, BRAIDS,

AND

HAIR JEWELRY OF EVERY DESCRIPTION.

Compiled from Original Designs and the Latest Parisian Patterns

BY

MARK CAMPBELL.

NEW YORK: M. CAMPBELL, 737 BROADWAY.

CHICAGO: 81 SOUTH CLARK STREET.

MDCCCLXVII.

Entered according to Act of Congress, in the year 1867, by

MARK CAMPBELL,

In the Clerk's Office of the District Court of the United States, for the Northern District of Illinois.

PREFACE.

The necessity for a comprehensive work, giving a full and detailed explanation of the Art of manufacturing Hair Work in all its various branches, has been so frequently urged upon the attention of the author, that, in compliance with an almost universal demand, he has concluded to publish a book which will clearly illustrate the Art of Hair Dressing, and making Hair Jewelry and Hair Work of every description. His perfect familiarity with the business--the result of many years' successful experience--renders him eminently competent to impart the fullest information upon the subject of which he treats, while the great consumption and rapidly increasing demand for every description of Hair Goods, will make this work he now presents to the public, one of particular interest to all classes. Heretofore the Art of making these goods has been zealously guarded by a few dealers, who have accumulated fortunes, and would still retain it a profound secret but for the publication of this book. This is the only descriptive volume ever published on Hair Work. It is an elaborate, carefully prepared book, containing over one thousand drawings, devices and diagrams, engraved at great expense to the publisher, and accompanied with the most comprehensive instructions. It not only reveals to the most ordinary comprehension the hitherto concealed mysteries of the Art, but will prove an indispensable adjunct to every lady's toilet table, as by its aid she will not only be able to dress her own hair in every variety of style, but make her own Hair Jewelry and articles of Hair work, including Switches, Braids, Curls, Waterfalls, &c., assisted by a reference to plates of the most modern European and American styles. For children, no art or accomplishment is more useful than the ability to make articles of tasteful ornament in Hair Work. This work will open to all such persons a path to agreeable and profitable occupation. Jewelry Dealers, from the clear instructions herein given, can manufacture any required pattern of Hair Jewelry, and add, without extra expense, a new and lucrative branch to their business.

Persons wishing to preserve and weave into lasting mementos, the hair of a deceased father, mother, sister, brother, or child, can also enjoy the inexpressible advantage and satisfaction of knowing that the material of their own handiwork is the actual hair of the "loved and gone."

No other work ever met with such an earnest demand as this treatise upon the art of Hair Braiding. It must certainly commend itself to the ladies of our country as invaluable. Even a hasty perusal will convince every one of its utility and worth. Translations in French and German are in progress.

INTRODUCTORY REMARKS.

IN this book of instruction, I have introduced for practice the easiest braids first--which are chain braids. The first pattern, found on page 9, is a very easy and handsome one, and should be practiced to perfection before trying any other, as it will enable the beginner to execute all others after the first is perfected. A new beginner should be particular to place the strands correctly upon the table, and mark the cover with precision, after the manner shown in the diagram. I have, by the introduction of plates, diagrams and explanatory remarks, made comprehensive and simple the execution of all the braids herein contained. The novice should first give special attention to preparing the hair for braiding, the adjustment of it to the bobbins, weights, molds, &c., of which plates, and full explanations are to be found elsewhere in this book. I wish to impress upon the mind of the worker, that every change made with the strands changes the numbers of them to correspond with the numbers on the table. For example: lift No. 1 over No. 2, which would make No. 1 No. 2, and No. 2 No. 1, &c.

SQUARE CHAIN BRAID.

TAKE sixteen strands, eighty hairs in a strand, and place on table like pattern. Commence at A, take Nos. 1,--one in each hand--lift them over the table, one on each side of the mold, and lay them between Nos. 1 at B, and bring back the Nos. 2 from B, one on each side of the mold, and lay them between Nos. 2 at A; then go to C, lift Nos. 1 over between Nos. 1 at D, passing one strand each side of the mold, and bring back Nos. 2 from D, and lay between Nos. 2 at C. Then you are through the braid, ready to commence at A, as at first, and repeat until finished.

Braid this over a mold, made of small wire, with a hole in one end like the eye of a needle, so as to draw a small cord in the place of the wire. When you have it braided, take off the weights, tie the ends fast on the wire, and push the braid tight together; then boil in water about ten minutes, and take it out and put in an oven as hot as it will bear without burning, until quite dry; then slip it off the wire on to the cord, sew the ends of the braid so it will not slip, and put a little shellac on the end to keep it fast. If you want it elastic, use elastic cord. To vary the size of the braid, vary the number of hairs in a strand.

REVERSE CHAIN BRAID.

TAKE sixteen strands and place on table like pattern. Commence at A with sixty hairs in a strand. Take Nos. 2, lift over table to B, lay them in between Nos. 1 at B, and bring back Nos. 2 from B, and lay in between Nos. 1 at A. Then walk around table to C; take Nos. 1 and lift over table and lay them in between Nos. 1 at D, and bring back Nos. 1 from D to C; then take Nos. 2 at C, lift over table and lay them inside of Nos. 2 at D, and bring back Nos. 2 from D to C. After braiding several times round to suit your taste, say five, reverse the braid by commencing at C, and braiding as you did at A, by taking Nos. 2 at C, lift over table to D, and lay them in between Nos. 1 at D, and bring back Nos. 2 from D, and lay in between Nos. 1 at C. Then go to A and take Nos. 1, lift over table and lay in between Nos. 1 at B, and bring back Nos. 1 from B to A, then take Nos. 2 at A, lift over table and lay in between Nos. 2 at B, and fetch back Nos. 2 from B to A, then commence at C again and braid five times. Then commence at A as you did at first, reversing it every time you braid it five times through. Braid it over a small wire, tie the ends on the wire, boil and dry the same as chain on page nine, only you need not press the braid together on the wire.

SIXTEEN TWIST CHAIN.

TAKE sixteen strands, with eighty hairs in a strand, and place on table like pattern. Commence at A and B; take No. 1 at A in right hand, and No. 1 at B in left hand, and swing them around the table to the right, changing places with them. Then take Nos. 1 at C and D and change as at A and B. Then go to B and take Nos. 2 at B and A, and change them by taking No. 2 at B in right hand and No. 2 at A in left hand, and swing them around table to the right as before, changing places with them. Then go around the table to D, and take Nos. 2 at D and C, and change places as before, then take Nos. 3 at A and B and change as before. Then take Nos. 3 at C and D and change places with them. Then take Nos. 4 at B and A and change as before. Then take Nos. 4 at D and C and change as before. Then commence at A, as at first, repeating until the braid is finished.

STRIPED SNAKE CHAIN BRAID.

TAKE thirty-two strands with twelve hairs in a strand, or any number that can be divided by four, and sixty strands for usual size, and place them on table like pattern. Have every alternate two strands of black hair, and the others of light hair. Commence at A, taking two strands of light hair in left hand, Nos. 1 and 2, and take two strands of black hair in right hand, Nos. 3 and 4, and cross No. 2 (light) over No. 3 (dark), then No. 1 (light) under No. 3 (dark), then No. 4 (dark) over Nos. 1 and 2 (light); so on around the table to the right until you get to A; then commence and work back to the left by taking light hair in left hand and dark hair in right hand, as before, and put No. 3 (dark) over No. 2 (light), and No. 4 (dark) under No. 2 (light), and No. 1 (light) over Nos. 3 and 4 (dark), so on around the table till you get to A; then commence as at first, so on, braiding first one way around the table then the other till you have the chain completed.

Braid it over wood, or brass wire, the size and length you wish your chain. When braided take off your weights, tie the ends fast and boil and dry, then take out the mold and put a cord through with some cotton wrapped around it so it will be soft and pliable. This is called the STRIPED SNAKE BRAID, and can be braided all of one color if desired.

CABLE CHAIN BRAID.

TAKE any number of strands that can be divided by two, eighty hairs in a strand, twenty strands for usual size, place on table like pattern. Commencing, take No. 1 at A in right hand and No. 1 at B in left hand, and swing around the table to the right, and lay the one in right hand at No. 1 at B, and the one in left hand at No. 1 at A; then bring back No. 2 at B with right hand, and No. 2 at A in left hand, to the left, then take No. 3 and swing to the right, then No. 4 and swing to the left, so on, round first to the right then to the left, with every number of strands till you get to No. 1; then commence as at first, and so on till the chain is as long as required.

Braid this over a small wire, with a hole in one end like the eye of a needle, so as to draw a small cord in the place of the wire. When you have it braided take off your weights, tie the ends fast on the wire, and push the braid together on the wire; boil in water about ten minutes, then take it out and put it in an oven as hot as it will bear without burning, until it is quite dry; then take it out and slip off the wire on to the cord, and sew the ends of the braid so it will not slip on the cord, and put a little shellac on the end to keep it fast. If you want it elastic, use elastic cord. To vary the size of the braid, vary the number of hairs in a strand.

SNAKE CHAIN BRAID.

TAKE thirty-two strands, or any number that can be divided by four, twelve hairs in a strand, and sixty strands for usual size; place them on table like pattern. Commence at A, lift No. 2 in your right hand, and put your left under your right hand and take up No. 3 and bring it back of No. 1, and lay them both down; then take No. 4 up and lay it between Nos. 1 and 2, then take the next four to the right, and so on till you get around the table; then commence and braid back around the table to the left, but reverse the braid by braiding it this way: lift No. 3 with your left hand, pass your right under and take No. 2 and bring it back over No. 4, and lay them both down; then take No. 1 and lift it over in between Nos. 3 and 4, and so on, till you get around the table. Then commence as at first, braid one way, then the other, till you have it as long as required. Braid it over wood or brass wire the size and length you wish your chain; when braided take off your weights, tie the ends fast, and boil and dry them; take out the mold and put a cord through with some cotton wrapped around it so that it will be soft and pliable. This is called the SNAKE CHAIN BRAID.

EIGHT SQUARE CHAIN BRAID.

TAKE sixteen strands, eighty hairs in a strand, and place them on the table like pattern. Commence at A, take Nos. 1 strands, lift across the table and lay down inside of Nos. 1 at B, and bring back Nos. 1 from B to A, then lift Nos. 2 at A over inside Nos. 2 at B and bring Nos. 2 from B to A, then lift Nos. 3 from A to B, and bring back Nos. 3 from B to A, then lift Nos. 4 from A to B and bring back Nos. 4 from B to A, then commence at Nos. 1 again and repeat until the chain is completed.

Braid this over a small wire, with a hole in one end like the eye of an needle, so as to draw a small cord in the place of the wire. When you have it braided, take off your weights, tie the ends fast on the wire and push the braid together on the wire; then boil in water about ten minutes; then take it out and put in an oven as hot as it will bear without burning, until it is quite dry; then take it out and slip it off of the wire on to the cord, and sew the ends of the braid so it will not slip on the cord, and put a little shellac on the end to keep it fast. If you want it elastic, use elastic cord. To vary the size of the braid, vary the number of hairs in a strand.

HALF-TWIST CHAIN BRAID.

TAKE sixteen strands or any number that can be divided by two, usually eighty hairs in a strand. Commence at A and B, take No. 1 at A in right hand, and No. 1 at B in left hand, and swing them around table to right, and lay the one in right hand down at B across over No. 2, and the one in right hand lay down across over No. 2 at A; then go to C and D, and change No. 1 as before at A and B; then go to the next two strands and change as before, so on around the table, taking the next two each time until the chain is completed. Directions same as on page 9.

SQUARE CHAIN BRAID.

TAKE sixteen strands, eighty hairs in a strand, and place on table like pattern. Commence at A, lift Nos. 1 across table and lay in between Nos. 1 at B, and bring back Nos. 1 from B to A; then go to C, take Nos. 1 and lift across table and lay in between Nos. 1 at D, and bring back Nos. 1 from D to C; then go to A, take Nos. 2 and lift across inside of Nos. 2 at B, and bring back Nos. 2 from B to A; then go to C, lift Nos. 2 across inside of Nos. 2 at D, and bring back Nos. 2 from D to C; then go to A and commence as at first, and repeat until it is the required length.

Braid this over a small wire, with a hole in one end like the eye of a needle, so as to draw a small cord in the place of the wire. When you have it braided, take off your weights, tie the ends fast on the wire, and push the braid close together; then boil in water about ten minutes, and take it out and put it in an oven as hot as it will bear without burning, until it is quite dry; then take it out and slip it off the wire on to the cord, sew the ends of the braid so it will not slip, and put a little shellac on the ends to keep it fast. If you want it elastic, use elastic cord. To vary the size of the braid, vary the number of hairs in a strand.

CABLE TWIST CHAIN BRAID.

TAKE sixteen strands, eighty hairs in a strand, and place them on table like pattern. Commence at A and B with Nos. 1, passing them around table to the right, and leave No. 1 from A at B, and No. 1 from B at A. Then take Nos. 7 at A and B, and pass around table to right, and leave the one from A at B, and the one from B at A. Then take Nos. 2 at A and B, changing places with them; then take Nos. 8 and change as before; then take Nos. 3 at A and B and change them as before; then take Nos. 1 at A and B and change as at first;

then take Nos. 4 and change as before; then take Nos. 2 and change as before; then take Nos. 5 and change as before, so on until the braid is finished, all the time taking the third strand to the right, or forward, and the second one to the left, or backward.

Braid this over a small wire, with a hole in one end like the eye of a needle, so as to draw a small cord in the place of the wire. When you have it braided, take off your weights, tie the ends fast on the wire and push the braid together on the wire; then boil in water about ten minutes; then take it out and put in an oven as hot as it will bear without burning, until it is quite dry; then take it out and slip it off of the wire on to the cord, and sew the ends of the braid so it will not slip on the cord, and put a little shellac on the end to keep it fast. If you want it elastic, use elastic cord. To vary the size of the braid, vary the number of hairs in a strand.

TWIST CHAIN BRAID.

TAKE eighteen strands, eighty hairs in a strand, and place on table like pattern. Commence at A and B, take Nos. 1 and swing around table to the right, and place the No. 1 from A over the Nos. 2 and 3 at B, and the No. 1 from B over the Nos. 2 and 3 at A; then go to C and D, take the Nos. 1 and change the same; then go to E and F and change the same; then go to B and A, and change as at first,--all the time taking the Nos. 1, and swinging to the right, for when you lay them over the Nos. 2 and 3 it makes them Nos. 3, and makes Nos. 2 Nos. 1--and so on, until the chain is finished.

Braid this over a small wire, with a hole in one end like the eye of a needle, so as to draw a small cord in the place of the wire. When you have it braided, take off your weights, tie the ends fast on the wire, and push the braid close together; then boil in water about ten minutes, and take it out and put it in an oven as hot as it will bear without burning, until it is quite dry; then take it out and slip it off the wire on to the cord, sew the ends of the braid so it will not slip, and put a little shellac on the ends to keep it fast. If you want it elastic, use elastic cord. To vary the size of the braid, vary the number of hairs in a strand.

TWIST CHAIN BRAID.

TAKE sixteen strands, eighty hairs in a strand, and place them on table like pattern. Commence at A and B, take No. 1 at A in right hand and No. 1 at B in left hand and swing them around the table to the right and lay the one in the right hand down at B, over across Nos. 2, 3 and 4, and the one in the left hand at A over across Nos. 2, 3 and 4, then go to C and take No. 1 at C and D and change as before at A and B; then go to B and take No. 1 at B and A and change them by taking No. 1 at B in right hand, and No. 1 at A in left hand and swing them round the table to the right as before, laying them across over Nos. 2, 3 and 4; so on braiding around the table to the right until you have it the required length.

Braid this over a small wire, with a hole in one end like the eye of a needle, so as to draw a small cord in the place of the wire. When you have it braided, take off your weights, tie the ends fast on the wire and push the braid together on the wire; then boil in water about ten minutes; then take it out and put in an oven as hot as it will bear without burning, until it is quite dry; then take it out and slip it off of the wire on to the cord, and sew the ends of the braid so it will not slip on the cord, and put a little shellac on the end to keep it fast. If you want it elastic, use elastic cord. To vary the size of the braid, vary the number of hairs in a strand.

RIB CHAIN BRAID.

TAKE sixteen strands, eighty hairs in a strand, and place them on table like pattern. Commence at A, take Nos. 2 and lift over across table outside of Nos. 2 at B, and bring back Nos. 1 from B to A outside of Nos. 1 at A, then take Nos. 1 at C and cross over inside of Nos. 1 at D, and bring back Nos. 2 from D inside of Nos. 2 at C, then go back to A and braid as before, so on repeating until it is finished.

Braid this over a small wire, with a hole in one end like the eye of a needle, so as to draw a small cord in the place of the wire. When you have it braided, take off your weights, tie the ends fast on the wire and push the braid together on the wire; then boil in water about ten minutes; then take it out and put in an oven as hot as it will bear without burning, until it is quite dry; then take it out and slip it off of the wire on to the cord, and sew the ends of the braid so it will not slip on the cord, and put a little shellac on the end to keep it fast. If you want it elastic, use elastic cord. To vary the size of the braid, vary the number of hairs in a strand.

TWIST CHAIN BRAID.

TAKE ten strands, eighty hairs in a strand, and place them on the table like pattern. Commence at A and B, take Nos. 1 and swing them around the table to the right, and leave No. 1 from A at B and the No. 1 from B at A, then take the Nos. 2 and swing them around the table to the right and change places with each other, then take Nos. 3 and change places as before; then take Nos. 4 and change places as before; then take Nos. 5 and change places as before; then commence at Nos. 1 and repeat until the braid is finished.

Braid this over a small wire, with a hole in one end like the eye of a needle, so as to draw a small cord in the place of the wire. When you have it braided, take off your weights, tie the ends fast on the wire and push the braid together on the wire; then boil in water about ten minutes; then take it out and put in an oven as hot as it will bear without burning, until it is quite dry; then take it out and slip it off of the wire on to the cord, and sew the ends of the braid so it will not slip on the cord, and put a little shellac on the end to keep it fast. If you want it elastic, use elastic cord. To vary the size of the braid, vary the number of hairs in a strand.

HALF TWIST CHAIN BRAID.

TAKE sixteen strands, seventy-five hairs in a strand, and place on the table like pattern. Commence at A take Nos. 1 and 2, lift across the table to B, and lay No. 1 outside of No. 4, and lay No. 2 between Nos. 1 and 2, and bring back Nos. 1 and 2 from B to A, and lay No. 1 outside of No. 4, and No. 2 outside of No. 1 at A; then go to C and take Nos. 1 and 2, lift over table to D and lay No. 1 outside of No. 4, and lay No. 2 between Nos. 1 and 2, and bring back Nos. 1 and 2 from C, and lay No. 1 outside of No. 4, and No. 2 outside of No. 1 at C; then go to B and change the same, and so on around the table to the right until the braid is finished.

Braid this over a small wire, with a hole in one end like the eye of a needle, so as to draw a small cord in the place of the wire. When you have it braided, take off your weights, tie the ends fast on the wire and push the braid together on the wire; then boil in water about ten minutes; then take it out and put in an oven as hot as it will bear without burning, until it is quite dry; then take it out and slip it off of the wire on to the cord, and sew the ends of the braid so it will not slip on the cord, and put a little shellac on the end to keep it fast. If you want it elastic, use elastic cord. To vary the size of the braid, vary the number of hairs in a strand.

CABLE CHAIN BRAID.

TAKE twenty strands, seventy-five hairs in a strand, place on table like pattern. Commence at A, lift Nos. 1 over across the table inside of Nos. 1 at B, and bring back Nos. 1 from B to A; then take Nos. 2 at A, cross over and lay them between Nos. 2 at B, and carry back Nos. 2 from B to A; then take Nos. 3 at A, cross over inside of Nos. 3 at B, and bring back Nos. 3 from B to A; then take Nos. 4 at A and cross over inside of Nos. 4 at B, and bring back Nos. 4 from B to A; then take Nos. 5 at A, cross over inside of Nos. 5 at B, and bring back Nos. 5 from B to A; then take Nos. 1 at B, cross over inside of Nos. 1 at A, and bring back Nos. 1 from A to B; then take Nos. 2 at B and cross over inside of Nos. 2 at A, and bring back Nos. 2 from A to B; then take Nos. 3, so on around the table to the right until the braid is finished, all the time taking the next two.

Braid this over a small wire, with a hole in one end like the eye of a needle, so as to draw a small cord in the place of the wire. When you have it braided, take off your weights, tie the ends fast on the wire and push the braid together on the wire; then boil in water about ten minutes; then take it out and put in an oven as hot as it will bear without burning, until it is quite dry; then take it out and slip it off of the wire on to the cord, and sew the ends of the braid so it will not slip on the cord, and put a little shellac on the end to keep it fast. If you want it elastic, use elastic cord. To vary the size of the braid, vary the number of hairs in a strand.

SIXTEEN SQUARE CHAIN BRAID.

TAKE thirty-two strands, fifty hairs in a strand, and place on table like pattern. Commence at A, lift Nos. 1 across inside of Nos. 1 at B, and bring back Nos. 1 from B to A; then change at C and D, E and F, and G and H the same, then go to A, lift Nos. 2 across in place of Nos. 2 at B, and bring back Nos. 2 from B to A; then change at C and D, E and F, and G and H the same. Then you are through the braid, ready to commence at A, as at first, repeating the changes until the braid is finished.

Braid this over a small wire, with a hole in one end like the eye of a needle, so as to draw a small cord in the place of the wire. When you have it braided, take off your weights, tie the ends fast on the wire, and push the braid close together; then boil in water about ten minutes, and take it out and put it in an oven as hot as it will bear without burning, until it is quite dry; then take it out and slip it off the wire on to the cord, sew the ends of the braid so it will not slip, and put a little shellac on the ends to keep it fast. If you want it elastic, use elastic cord. To vary the size of the braid, vary the number of hairs in a strand.

GERMAN TWIST CHAIN BRAID.

TAKE sixteen strands, eighty hairs in a strand, and place them on the table like pattern. Commence at A and B, take No. 1 at A in right hand and No. 1 at B in left hand, and swing them around to the right and change places with them; then take No. 1 at C in right hand and No. 1 at D in left hand, and swing around table to the right and change places as before; then take No. 2 at B in right hand and No. 2 at A in left hand and swing to the right and change as before; then take No. 2 at D in right hand and No. 2 at C in left hand and swing to the right and change as before; then take No. 3 at A in right hand and No. 3 at B in left hand and change as before; then take No. 3 at C in right hand and No. 3 at D in left hand and change as before; then take No. 4 at B in right hand and No. 4 at A in left hand and change as before then take No. 4 at D in right hand and No. 4 at C in left hand and change as before. Then commence at A as at first and repeat till the braid is finished.

FANCY SQUARE CHAIN BRAID.

TAKE twenty-four strands, seventy hairs in a strand, and place on table like pattern. Commence at A--change Nos. 1 at A across inside of Nos. 1 at B, and bring back Nos. 1 from B to A, then go to C, change Nos. 1 across inside of Nos. 1 at D, and bring back Nos. 1 from D to C, then take Nos. 1 at E in right hand and No. 1 at F in left hand, lift across table in place of Nos. 1 at G and H, and bring back Nos. 1 from G and H to F and E; then take Nos. 2 at E and F and change across to G and H, and lay in place of Nos. 2, and bring back Nos. 2 from G and H to F and E; then take Nos 3 and change across to G and H as before; then take Nos. 4 at F and E and change across to G and H as before; then go to C and change the Nos. 1 across to D, and bring the Nos. 1 from D to C; then go to A and change the Nos. 1 across to B, and bring back Nos. 1 from B to A; then go to E and H, take No. 4 at H in right hand, and No. 4 at E in left hand, and lift across in place of Nos. 4 at F and G, and bring back Nos. 4 from F and G to E and H; then take Nos. 3 at E and H and change across in place of Nos. 3 at F and G, and bring back Nos. 3 from F and G to E and H; then take Nos. 2 at E and H and change across in place of Nos. 2 at F and G and bring back Nos. 2 from F and G to E and H; then take Nos. 1 at E and H, and change across in place of Nos. 1 at F and G, and bring back Nos. 1 from F and G to E and H; then go to A and commence as at first, and repeat till the chain is finished.

FANCY SQUARE CHAIN BRAID.

TAKE twenty-four strands, seventy hairs in a strand, and place on table like pattern. Commence at A, lift Nos. 1 across inside of No. 1 at B, and bring back Nos. 1 from B to A; then change Nos. 1 at C and D the same; then change Nos. 1 at E and F the same; then go to A, lift Nos. 2 across to B, and bring back Nos. 2 from B to A; then change Nos. 2 at C and D the same; then change Nos. 2 at E and F the same, and you are through the braid ready to commence at A as at first.

Braid this over a small wire, with a hole in one end like the eye of a needle, so as to draw a small cord in the place of the wire. When you have it braided, take off your weights, tie the ends fast on the wire and push the braid together on the wire; then boil in water about ten minutes; then take it out and put in an oven as hot as it will bear without burning, until it is quite dry; then take it out and slip it off of the wire on to the cord, and sew the ends of the braid so it will not slip on the cord and put a little shellac on the end to keep it fast. If you want it elastic, use elastic cord. To vary the size of the braid, vary the number of hairs in a strand.

SQUARE CHAIN BRAID.

TAKE sixteen strands, eighty hairs in a strand, and place them on the table like pattern. Commence at A, change the Nos. 1 across inside of Nos. 1 at B, and bring back Nos. 1 from B to A; then take No. 2 at A change over in place of Nos. 2 at B and bring back Nos. 2 from B to A; then go to C, and change the Nos. 1 from C to D, and bring back Nos. 1 from D to C; then take Nos. 2 at C and change over in place of Nos. 2 at D, and bring back Nos 2 from D to C; then go to A and begin as at first, repeating until the braid is finished.

Braid this over a small wire, with a hole in one end like the eye of a needle, so as to draw a small cord in the place of the wire. When you have it braided, take off your weights, tie the ends fast on the wire and push the braid together on the wire; then boil in water about ten minutes; then take it out and put in an oven as hot as it will bear without burning, until it is quite dry, then take it out and slip it off of the wire on to the cord, and sew the ends of the braid so it will not slip on the cord, and put a little shellac on the end to keep it fast. If you want it elastic, use elastic cord. To vary the size of the braid, vary the number of hairs in a strand.

FANCY TWIST CHAIN BRAID.

TAKE thirty-two strands, fifty hairs in a strand, and place on table like pattern. Change Nos. 1 at A across inside of Nos. 1 at B, and bring back Nos. 1 from B to A; then change in the same way, successively, the Nos. 3, 5, 2, 4, 6, 3, 5, 7, 4, 6, 8, 5, 7, 1, 6, 8, 2, 7, 1, 3, 8, 2, 4--then you are through, ready to commence as at first.

Braid this over a small wire, with a hole in one end like the eye of a needle, so as to draw a small cord in the place of the wire. When you have it braided, take off your weights, tie the ends fast on the wire and push the braid together on the wire, then boil in water about ten minutes; then take it out and put in an oven as hot as it will bear without burning, until it is quite dry; then take it out and slip it off of the wire on to the cord, and sew the ends of the braid so it will not slip on the cord, and put a little shellac on the end to keep it fast. If you want it elastic, use elastic cord. To vary the size of the braid, vary the number of hairs in a strand.

FANCY TWIST CHAIN BRAID.

TAKE sixteen strands, eighty hairs in a strand, and lay on table like pattern. Commence at A and B--take No. 1 at A in left hand and No. 1 at B in right hand, swing around table to the left, and change places with them; then take No. 7 at B in right hand and No. 7 at A in left hand, and swing around the table to the right and change places with them; then take No. 5 at A in right hand and No. 5 at B in left hand, and swing around the table to the left, and change places as before; then take No. 8 at A in right hand and No. 8 at B in left hand and swing around table to the left and change as before; then take

No. 6 at A in left hand, and No. 6 at B in right hand and swing around table to the right and change as before; then take No. 4 at A in right hand and No. 4 at B in left hand, and swing around table to the left and change as before; then take No. 7 at A in right hand and No. 7 at B in left hand, swing around table to the left and change as before, then take No. 5 at A in left hand and No. 5 at B in right hand, swing around table to the right and change as before; then take No. 3 at A in right hand and No. 3 at B in left hand and swing around table to the left and change as before; then take No. 6 at A in right hand and No. 6 at B in left hand and swing around table to the left and change as before; then take No. 4 at A in left hand and No. 4 at B in right hand and swing around table to the right and change as before; then take No. 2 at A in right hand and No. 2 at B in left hand and swing around table to the left and change as before; then take No. 5 at A in right hand and No. 5 at B in left hand and swing around table to the left and change as before, then take No. 3 at A in left hand and No. 3 at B in right hand, and swing around table to the right and change as before. Then commence at A as at first.

Braid this over a small wire, with a hole in one end like the eye of a needle, so as to draw a small cord in the place of the wire. When you have it braided, take off your weights, tie the ends fast on the wire and push the braid together on the wire; then boil in water about ten minutes; then take it out and put in an oven as hot as it will bear without burning, until it is quite dry; then take it out and slip it off of the wire on to the cord, and sew the ends of the braid so it will not slip on the cord, and put a little shellac on the end to keep it fast. If you want it elastic, use elastic cord. To vary the size of the braid, vary the number of hairs in a strand.

DOUBLE TWIST CHAIN BRAID.

TAKE eighteen strands, eighty hairs in a strand, and place on table like pattern. Commence at A and B--take No. 1 at A in right hand and No. 1 at B in left hand and swing them around the table to the right and change places with them; then change the Nos. 8, 6 and 4 the same way; then count back five to the left (not counting the one last braided), bringing you to No. 9--

swing as before to the right and change places; then change the Nos. 7, 5 and 3 the same way; then count back five, bringing you to No. 8--change the same; and so on, first counting two forward and change three times, and then count five back and change the same, so on until the braid is finished.

Braid this over a small wire, with a hole in one end like the eye of a needle, so as to draw a small cord in the place of the wire. When you have it braided, take off your weights, tie the ends fast on the wire and push the braid together on the wire; then boil in water about ten minutes; then take it out and put in an oven as hot as it will bear without burning, until it is quite dry; then take it out and slip it off of the wire on to the cord, and sew the ends of the braid so it will not slip on the cord, and put a little shellac on the end to keep it fast. If you want it elastic, use elastic cord. To vary the size of the braid, vary the number of hairs in a strand.

FANCY CABLE CHAIN BRAID.

TAKE sixteen strands, eighty hairs in a strand, and place them on the table like pattern. Commence at A and B, take No. 1 at A in right hand and No. 1 at B in left hand, and swing them around to the left and change places with them; then take successively Nos. 3, 5, 2, 4, 6, 3, 5, 7, 4, 6, 8, and change the same; then commence as at first with No. 1, so on repeating until the braid is finished.

Braid this over a small wire, with a hole in one end like the eye of a needle, so as to draw a small cord in the place of the wire. When you have it braided, take off your weights, tie the ends fast on the wire and push the braid together on the wire; then boil in water about ten minutes; then take it out and put in an oven as hot as it will bear without burning, until it is quite dry then take it out and slip it off of the wire on to the cord, and sew the ends of the braid so it will not slip on the cord, and put a little shellac on the end to keep it fast. If you want it elastic, use elastic cord. To vary the size of the braid, vary the number of hairs in a strand.

HALF SQUARE CHAIN BRAID.

TAKE twenty four strands, seventy hairs in a strand, and arrange like pattern. Commence at A, take Nos. 1 and lay them in the place of Nos. 1 at B, and bring back Nos. 1 from B to A; then take Nos. 2 at C and lay in the place of Nos. 2 at D and bring back Nos. 2 from D to C. Then take the Nos. 3 from H and lay between the Nos. 3 at G, and bring back the Nos. 3 from G to H; then take the Nos. 4 at H and place between the Nos. 4 at G, and bring back the Nos. 4 from G to H; then take Nos. 5 at E and place between Nos. 5 at F, and bring back the Nos. 5 from F to E; then take the Nos. 6 at E and place them inside of Nos. 6 at F, and bring back the Nos. 6 from F to E. Commence at A as at first, and repeat until the braid is finished.

Braid this over a small wire, with a hole in one end like the eye of a needle, so as to draw a small cord in the place of the wire. When you have it braided, take off your weights, tie the ends fast on the wire and push the braid together on the wire; then boil in water about ten minutes; then take it out and put in an oven as hot as it will bear without burning, until it is quite dry; then take it out and slip it off of the wire on to the cord, and sew the ends of the braid so it will not slip on the cord, and put a little shellac on the end to keep it fast. If you want it elastic, use elastic cord. To vary the size of the braid, vary the number of hairs in a strand.

TWELVE SQUARE CHAIN BRAID.

TAKE twenty-four strands, and place on table like pattern. Commence at A, take Nos. 1 and place between Nos. 1 at B, and bring back Nos. 1 from B and lay in place of Nos. 1 at A; then change the Nos. 2 at A, and B the same way; then change the succeeding numbers, 3, 4, 5 and 6, all the same way. Then you are through the braid, ready to commence at Nos. 1 again, as at first, and repeat until the braid is the desired length.

Braid this over a small wire, with a hole in one end like the eye of a needle, so as to draw a small cord in the place of the wire. When you have it braided, take off your weights, tie the ends fast on the wire, and push the braid close together; then boil in water about ten minutes, and take it out and put it in an oven as hot as it will bear without burning, until it is quite dry; then take it out and slip it off the wire on to the cord, sew the ends of the braid so it will not slip, and put a little shellac on the ends to keep it fast. If you want it elastic, use elastic cord. To vary the size of the braid, vary the number of hairs in a strand.

FLAT TWIST CHAIN BRAID.

TAKE eight strands, ninety hairs in a strand, and place on table like pattern. Commence, take No. 1 at A in right hand, and No. 1 at B in left hand, and swing around table to the right--the No. 1 in the right hand over across Nos. 2, 3 and 4 at B, and the No. 1 in the left hand over across Nos. 2, 3 and 4 at A; repeat until the braid is finished.

Braid this over a small wire, with a hole in one end like the eye of a needle, so as to draw a small cord in the place of the wire. When you have it braided, take off your weights, tie the ends fast on the wire and push the braid together on the wire; then boil in water about ten minutes; then take it out and put in an oven as hot as it will bear without burning, until it is quite dry; then take it out and slip it off of the wire on to the cord, and sew the ends of the braid so it will not slip on the cord, and put a little shellac on the end to keep it fast. If you want it elastic, use elastic cord. To vary the size of the braid, vary the number of hairs in a strand.

RIB CHAIN BRAID.

TAKE sixteen strands, eighty hairs in a strand, and place them on the table like pattern. Commence at A, take both No. 1 strands and cross over in between Nos. 1 on the opposite side to B, then bring back both Nos. 2 from B to A, and place them in between Nos. 2; then walk around table to C and braid it across table to D as before. Then commence at A and repeat until braid is finished.

Braid this over a small wire, with a hole in one end like the eye of a needle, so as to draw a small cord in the place of the wire. When you have it braided, take off your weights, tie the ends fast on the wire and push the braid together on the wire; then boil in water about ten minutes; then take it out and put in an oven as hot as it will bear without burning, until it is quite dry; then take it out and slip it off of the wire on to the cord, and sew the ends of the braid so it will not slip on the cord, and put a little shellac on the end to keep it fast. If you want it elastic, use elastic cord. To vary the size of the braid, vary the number of hairs in a strand.

FANCY CABLE CHAIN BRAID

TAKE any number of strands that can be divided by two, eight hairs in a strand, and place on table like pattern. Commence by taking No. 1 at A and B and change places by swinging them to the right; then take No. 2 at A and B and change places with them by swinging to the left; then take No. 3 at A and B and change places by swinging them to the right; then Nos. 4, and change places by swinging them to the left, and so on, swinging to the right and left alternately, until the braid is finished.

Braid this over a small wire, with a hole in one end like the eye of a needle, so as to draw a small cord in the place of the wire. When you have it braided, take off your weights, tie the ends fast on the wire and push the braid together on the wire; then boil in water about ten minutes; then take it out and put in an oven as hot as it will bear without burning, until it is quite dry; then take it out and slip it off of the wire on to the cord, and sew the ends of the braid so it will not slip on the cord, and put a little shellac on the end to keep it fast. If you want it elastic, use elastic cord. To vary the size of the braid, vary the number of hairs in a strand.

SQUARE CABLE CHAIN BRAID.

TAKE any number of strands that can be divided by two, eighty hairs in a strand, and place on table like pattern. Commence at A and B, take Nos. 1 and swing them around table to the right--No. 1 from A around to B across No. 2 at B, and No. 1 from B across No. 2 at A; then take Nos. 1 at C and D and change as before; then change the same at E and F and at B and A, so on around the table to the right until the chain is completed. Any number of strands can be used by increasing the number in each place, or by having three, four, five or six in a place, care being taken to cross all the strands. For instance, there are four strands, No. 1 must be crossed over all as you braid around the table. By adding strands a different braid is formed.

Braid this over a small wire, with a hole in one end like the eye of a needle, so as to draw a small cord in the place of the wire. When you have it braided, take off your weights, tie the ends fast on the wire and push the braid together on the wire; then boil in water about ten minutes; then take it out and put in an oven as hot as it will bear without burning, until it is quite dry; then take it out and slip it off of the wire on to the cord, and sew the ends of the braid so it will not slip on the cord, and put a little shellac on the end to keep it fast. If you want it elastic, use elastic cord. To vary the size of the braid, vary the number of hairs in a strand.

FOB CHAIN BRAID.

TAKE twenty strands, seventy hairs in a strand, and place on table like pattern. Commence at A, cross No. 1 in the right hand over the No. 1 in the left hand, and then go to B and cross No. 1 in the left hand over No. 1 in the right hand; then go back to A and take Nos. 1 and cross inside of Nos. 1 at B, and bring back Nos. 1 from B to A; then take Nos. 2 and change the same; then change Nos. 3 the same; then go to C and take Nos. 1 and cross inside of Nos. 2 at D, and bring back Nos. 1 from D and lay inside of Nos. 2 at C; then commence at A as at first, and repeat until the braid is finished.

Braid this over a small wire, with a hole in one end like the eye of a needle, so as to draw a small cord in the place of the wire. When you have it braided, take off your weights, tie the ends fast on the wire and push the braid together on the wire; then boil in water about ten minutes; then take it out and put in an oven as hot as it will bear without burning, until it is quite dry; then take it out and slip it off of the wire on to the cord, and sew the ends of the braid so it will not slip on the cord, and put a little shellac on the end to keep it fast. If you want it elastic, use elastic cord. To vary the size of the braid, vary the number of hairs in a strand.

SQUARE RIBBED CHAIN BRAID.

TAKE twenty strands, seventy hairs in a strand, and place on table like pattern. Commence take No. 1 at A in right hand and No. 1 at B in left hand, swing to the right and change places with them; then take Nos. 3 at A and lay inside of Nos. 2 at B, and bring Nos. 3 from B and lay inside of Nos. 2 at A; then go to C and take No. 1 in right hand and No. 1 at D in left hand, swing to the right and change places with them; then take Nos. 3 at C and lay inside of Nos. 2 at D, and bring back Nos. 3 from D and lay inside of Nos. 2 at C. Then commence at A as at first, and repeat until the braid is finished.

Braid this over a small wire, with a hole in one end like the eye of a needle, so as to draw a small cord in the place of the wire. When you have it braided, take off your weights, tie the ends fast on the wire and push the braid together on the wire; then boil in water about ten minutes; then take it out and put in an oven as hot as it will bear without burning, until it is quite dry, then take it out and slip it off of the wire on to the cord, and sew the ends of the braid so it will not slip on the cord, and put a little shellac on the end to keep it fast. If you want it elastic, use elastic cord. To vary the size of the braid, vary the number of hairs in a strand.

DOUBLE LOOP CHAIN BRAID.

TAKE twenty-four strands, sixty hairs in a strand, and place on table like pattern. Commence at A and B: take Nos. 1 at A, and lift them across the table, and lay the one in left hand between Nos. 1 at B, and the one in right hand on the outside of Nos. 1 at B, and bring back the Nos. 1 from B to A.

Then pass round the table to the right, and change (in the same manner) successively, the Nos. 3, 5, 6, 2, 4, 6, 2, 4, 5, 1, 3 and 5; then commence at A with Nos. 1, as at first, and repeat until the braid is finished.

Braid this over a small wire, with a hole in one end like the eye of a needle, so as to draw a small cord in the place of the wire. When you have it braided, take off your weights, tie the ends fast on the wire, and push the braid close together; then boil in water about ten minutes, and take it out and put it in an oven as hot as it will bear without burning, until it is quite dry; then take it out and slip it off the wire on to the cord, sew the ends of the braid so it will not slip, and put a little shellac on the ends to keep it fast. If you want it elastic, use elastic cord. To vary the size of the braid, vary the number of hairs in a strand.

KNOT CHAIN BRAID.

TAKE thirty-two strands with fifty hairs in a strand, and place them on table like pattern. Commence at A, take Nos. 4 and lift over across table, and lay outside of Nos. 1 at B, then bring back Nos. 4 from B and lay outside of Nos. 1 at A; then take Nos. 3 at A and lift over across table and lay outside of Nos. 1 at B, and bring back Nos. 3 from B and lay outside of Nos. 1 at A; then change Nos. 2 at A and B the same; then take Nos. 1 and change the same; then go to D and change the same as at A; then go to B and change the same; then go to C and change the same, and you are ready to commence again at A, as at first: repeat until braid is finished.

Braid this over a small wire, with a hole in one end like the eye of a needle, so as to draw a small cord in the place of the wire. When you have it braided, take off your weights, tie the ends fast on the wire and push the braid together on the wire; then boil in water about ten minutes; then take it out and put in an oven as hot as it will bear without burning, until it is quite dry; then take it out and slip it off of the wire on to the cord, and sew the ends of the braid so it will not slip on the cord, and put a little shellac on the end to keep it fast. If you want it elastic, use elastic cord. To vary the size of the braid, vary the number of hairs in a strand.

DOUBLE RIB CHAIN BRAID.

TAKE thirty-two strands, sixty hairs in a strand and place on table like pattern. Commence at A, take Nos. 4 and lift over table and lay outside of Nos. 1 at B, and bring back Nos. 4 from B and lay outside of Nos. 1 at A; then go to D and change the Nos. 4 the same as at A and B; then go to B and change the same as at A; then go to C and change the same way, and then to A and change as at first, and so on, repeating the changes until the braid is finished.

Braid this over a small wire, with a hole in one end like the eye of a needle, so as to draw a small cord in the place of the wire. When you have it braided, take off your weights, tie the ends fast on the wire, and push the braid close together; then boil in water about ten minutes, and take it out and put it in an oven as hot as it will bear without burning, until it is quite dry; then take it out and slip it off the wire on to the cord, sew the ends of the braid so it will not slip, and put a little shellac on the ends to keep it fast. If you want it elastic, use elastic cord. To vary the size of the braid, vary the number of hairs in a strand.

FANCY CHAIN BRAID.

TAKE sixteen strands eighty hairs in a strand, and place on table like pattern. Commence at A, change Nos. 1 across inside of Nos. 1 at B, and bring back Nos. 1 from B to A; then take Nos. 2 at A and change across inside of Nos. 2 at B, and bring back Nos. 2 from B to A; then go to C and change the Nos. 1 and the Nos. 2 across with the numbers at D the same as at A; then return to A and commence as at first and repeat ten times. Then change the figures on the table to correspond with the following diagram:

Then commence at A and B, take No. 1 at A in right hand and No. 1 at B in left hand, and swing around the table to the right, changing places with them; then take Nos. 1 at C and D and change the same; then change Nos. 2 at B and A the same; then change the Nos. 2 at D and C the same; then take Nos. 3 at A and B and change the same; then change the Nos. 3 at C and D; then the Nos. 4 at B and A; then the Nos. 4 at P and C; then commence at A as at first, and repeat ten times, so on braiding alternately ten rounds by the directions of each pattern until the braid is finished.

FANCY CHAIN BRAID.

TAKE sixteen strands eighty hairs in a strand, and place on table like pattern. Commence at A, change Nos. 1 across inside of Nos. 1 at B, and bring back Nos. 1 from B to A; then take Nos. 2 at A and change across inside of Nos. 2 at B, and bring back Nos. 2 from B to A; then go to C and change the Nos. 1 and the Nos. 2 across with the numbers at D the same as at A; then return to A and commence as at first and repeat ten times. Then change the figures on the table to correspond with the following diagram:

Then commence at A, take Nos. 1 and 2, lift across table to B and lay No. 1 outside of No. 4, and No. 2 between Nos. 1 and 2, and bring back Nos. 1 and 2 from B to A, and lay No. 1 outside of No. 4, and No. 2 outside of No. 1 at A; then go to C and take Nos. 1 and 2 and lift over table to D, and lay No. 1 outside of No. 4, and No. 2 between Nos. 1 and 2, and bring back Nos. 1 and 2 from C and lay No. 1 outside of No. 4 and No. 2 outside of No. 1 at C; then go to B and change the same, and so on around the table to the right, braiding alternately ten rounds by each diagram until the braid is finished.

FANCY CHAIN BRAID.

TAKE sixteen strands eighty hairs in a strand, and place them on table like pattern. Commence at A, lift Nos. 1 over across the table and lay them in between Nos. 1 at B, and bring back Nos. 1 from B to A; then go to C and change the Nos. 1 across with the Nos. 1 at D the same; then take Nos. 2 at A and change across inside of Nos. 2 at B, and bring back Nos. 2 from B to A; then change the Nos. 2 at C across inside of Nos. 2 at D the same; then commence at A as at first, and repeat ten times. Then change the numbers on table to correspond with the following pattern or diagram:

Then commence at A, take Nos. 1 and 2, lift across table to B and lay No. 1 outside of No. 4, and No. 2 between Nos. 1 and 2, and bring back Nos. 1 and 2 from B to A, and lay No. 1 outside of No. 4, and No. 2 outside of No. 1 at A; then go to C and take Nos. 1 and 2 and lift over table to D, and lay No. 1 outside of No. 4, and No. 2 between Nos. 1 and 2, and bring back Nos. 1 and 2 from C and lay No. 1 outside of No. 4 and No. 2 outside of No. 1 at C; then go to B and change the same, and so on around the table to the right, braiding alternately ten rounds by each diagram until the braid is finished.

FANCY CHAIN BRAID.

TAKE sixteen strands, eighty hairs in a strand, and place them on the table like pattern. Commence at A and B, take No. 1 at A in right hand and No. 1 at B in left hand, swing around the table to the right and change places with them; then take Nos. 1 at C and D and change as at A and B; then change Nos. 2 at B and A the same; then change the Nos. 2 at D and C the same; then take Nos. 3 at A and B and change the same; then change the Nos. 3 at C and D; then the Nos. 4 at B and A, and also the Nos. 4 at D and C, all the time swinging to the right. Braid around ten times.

Then commence at A, take Nos. 1 and 2, lift across table to B and lay No. 1 outside of No. 4, and No. 2 between Nos. 1 and 2, and bring back Nos. 1 and 2 from B to A, and lay No. 1 outside of No. 4, and No. 2 outside of No. 1 at A; then change the same at C, B and D; then commence again at A and braid ten rounds, so on braiding alternately ten rounds by the directions of each pattern until the braid is finished.

FANCY CHAIN BRAID.

TAKE sixteen strands eighty hairs in a strand, and place on table like pattern. Commence at A, change Nos. 1 across inside of Nos. 1 at B, and bring back Nos. 1 from B to A; then take Nos. 2 at A and change across inside of Nos. 2 at

B, and bring back Nos. 2 from B to A; then go to C and change the Nos. 1 and the Nos. 2 across with the numbers at D the same as at A; then return to A and commence as at first and repeat ten times. Then change the figures on the table to correspond with the following diagram:

[Illustration]

Then commence at A and B, take No. 1 at A in right hand and No. 1 at B in left hand, and swing them around the table to the right, and lay the one in right hand down at B over across Nos. 2, 3 and 4, and the one in left hand at A over across Nos. 2, 3 and 4; then go to C and change the Nos. 1 at B and D the same; then go to B and change the Nos. 1 at B and A the same; so on, braiding around the table to the right, alternately braiding ten rounds by the directions of each pattern until the braid is finished.

FANCY CHAIN BRAID.

TAKE sixteen strands, eighty hairs in a strand, and place them on table like pattern. Commence at A, lift Nos. 1 over across the table and lay them in between Nos. 1 at B, and bring back Nos. 1 from B to A; then go to C and change the Nos. 1 across with the Nos. 1 at D the same; then take Nos. 2 at A and change across inside of Nos. 2 at B, and bring back Nos. 2 from B to A; then change the Nos. 2 at C across inside of Nos. 2 at D the same; then commence at A as at first, and repeat ten times. Then change the numbers on table to correspond with the following pattern or diagram:

Then commence at A and B, take No. 1 at A in right hand and No. 1 at B in left hand, and swing them around the table to the right, and lay the one in right hand down at B over across Nos. 2, 3 and 4, and the one in left hand at A over across Nos. 2, 3 and 4; then go to C and change the Nos. 1 at B and D the same; then go to B and change the Nos. 1 at B and A the same; so on, braiding around the table to the right, alternately braiding ten rounds by the directions of each pattern until the braid is finished.

DOUBLE RIB CHAIN BRAID.

TAKE twenty-six strands, sixty hairs in a strand, and place on table like pattern. Commence at A and B, take Nos. 1 and change places by swinging them around the table to the left; then take the third strands to the right of A and B, and change places by swinging them around the table to the right; then take the fourth strands to the right of the ones last taken, and change places by swinging them around the table to the left, and so on working around the table to the right; first swinging the strands to the left, and then to the right, taking alternately the third and fourth strands to the right of the ones last used, until the braid is finished.

[Illustration]

Braid this over a small wire, with a hole in one end like the eye of a needle, so as to draw a small cord in the place of the wire. When you have it braided, take off your weights, tie the ends fast on the wire, and push the braid together; then boil in water about ten minutes, and then take out and put it in an oven as hot as it will bear without burning, until it is quite dry; then take it out and slip it off the wire and on the cord, and sew the ends so it will not slip, and put a little shellac on the end to keep it fast. If you want it elastic, use elastic cord. To vary the size of the braid vary the number of hairs in a strand.

ROPE CHAIN BRAID.

TAKE twenty-four strands, sixty hairs in a strand, and place on table like pattern. Commence at A, take No. 2 in right hand, swing around the table to the right and lay in place of No. 2 at B, and bring back No. 2 from B and lay in place of No. 2 at A; then take No. 1 at A in left hand, and change places with No. 1 at B by swinging around to the left; then go to C, take Nos. 3 and lift over table and lay inside of Nos. 3 at D, and bring back Nos. 3 from D and lay in place of Nos. 3 at C; then go to E and change the Nos. at E and F the same as at A and B; then go to G and change the same as at C and D, and so on, alternately changing, first as at A and B, and then as at C and D, until the braid is finished.

Braid this over a small wire, with a hole in one end like the eye of a needle, so as to draw a small cord in the place of the wire. When you have it braided, take off your weights, tie the ends fast on the wire, and push the braid together; then boil in water about ten minutes, and then take out and put it in an oven as hot as it will bear without burning, until it is quite dry; then take it out and slip it off the wire and on the cord, and sew the ends so it will not slip, and put a little shellac on the end to keep it fast. If you want it elastic, use elastic cord. To vary the size of the braid, vary the number of hairs in a strand.

DIAMOND SHAPED CHAIN BRAID.

TAKE twenty-four strands, seventy hairs in a strand, and place on the table like pattern. Commence at A, take Nos. 2 lift across table and lay in between Nos. 2 at B, and bring back Nos. 2 from B to A; then take Nos. 1 at A and lift across table and lay between Nos. 1 at B, and bring back Nos. 1 from B to A; then go to F, take No. 1 in right hand, swing around to the right and lay in place of No. 4 at E; then take No. 1 at E in left hand and swing around to the left and lay in place of No. 4 at F; then go to C, take Nos. 2 lift across table, and lay them in between Nos. 2 at D, and bring back Nos. 2 from D to C; then take Nos. 1 at C, lift across the table and lay between Nos. 1 at D, and bring back Nos. 1 from D to C; then you are through the braid, ready to commence as at first.

Braid this over a small wire, with a hole in one end like the eye of a needle, so as to draw a small cord in the place of the wire. When you have it braided, take off your weights, tie the ends fast on the wire, and push the braid together; then boil in water about ten minutes, and then take out and put it in an oven as hot as it will bear without burning, until it is quite dry; then take it out and slip it off the wire and on the cord, and sew the ends so it will not slip, and put a little shellac on the end to keep it fast. If you want it elastic, use elastic cord. To vary the size of the braid, vary the number of hairs in a strand.

FANCY SQUARE CHAIN BRAID.

TAKE twenty-four strands, eighty hairs in a strand, and place on table like pattern. Commence at A, take No. 1 in right hand, swing around to the right and lay in place of No. 4 at B; then take No. 1 at B in left hand, swing around table to the left and lay in place of No. 4 at A; then go to C, take No. 2 in right hand, swing around the table to the right and lay outside of No. 2 at D, and bring back No. 2 from D to C; then take No. 1 at C in left hand, swing around the table to the left and lay outside of No. 1 at D, and bring back No. 1 from D to C; then go to E and change the Nos. at E and F the same as you did at A and B; then change the Nos. at G and H the same as you did at C and D. Then you are through the braid, ready to commence at A, as at first.

Braid this over a small wire, with a hole in one end like the eye of a needle, so as to draw a small cord in the place of the wire. When you have it braided, take off your weights, tie the ends fast on the wire, and push the braid together; then boil in water about ten minutes, and then take out and put it in an oven as hot as it will bear without burning, until it is quite dry; then take it out and slip it off the wire and on the cord, and sew the ends so it will not slip, and put a little shellac on the end to keep it fast. If you want it elastic, use elastic cord. To vary the size of the braid, vary the number of hairs in a strand.

FANCY SQUARE CHAIN BRAID.

TAKE twenty-four strands, eighty hairs in a strand, and place on table like pattern. Commence at A, take No. 1 in right hand, swing around to the right and lay in place of No. 4 at B; then take No. 1 at B in left hand, swing around table to the left and lay in place of No. 4 at A; then go to C, take Nos. 1 and lift them across the table and lay in between Nos. 1 at D, and bring back Nos. 1 from D to C; then go to E, and change the Nos. at E and F the same as you did at A and B; then go to G, and change the Nos. at G and H the same as you did at C and D. Then you are through the braid, ready to commence at A, as at first.

Braid this over a small wire, with a hole in one end like the eye of a needle, so as to draw a small cord in the place of the wire. When you have it braided, take off your weights, tie the ends fast on the wire, and push the braid together; then boil in water about ten minutes, and then take out and put it in an oven as hot as it will bear without burning, until it is quite dry; then take it out and slip it off the wire and on the cord, and sew the ends so it will not slip, and put a little shellac on the end to keep it fast. If you want it elastic, use elastic cord. To vary the size of the braid, vary the number of hairs in a strand.

FANCY SQUARE CHAIN BRAID

TAKE twenty-four strands, eighty hairs in a strand, and place on table like pattern. Commence at A, take No. 1 at the left side of A in the right hand, and No. 1 at the left of B in the left hand, swing them around the table to the right and lay the one from B at the right of A, and the one from A at the right of B; then go to C, take No. 1 at the left side of C in the right hand, and No. 1 at the left side of D in the left hand, swing them around the table to the right, and lay the one from C at the right of D, and the one from D at the right of C; then go to B, take Nos. 3 and lift them across table and lay between Nos. 3 at A, and bring back Nos. 3 from A to B; then change Nos. 2 and 1 the same way; then go to C, take Nos. 3 and lift across the table and lay between Nos. 3 at D, and bring back Nos. 3 from D to C; then change Nos. 2 and 1 the same way. Then you are through the braid, ready to commence as at first, at A.

FANCY SQUARE CHAIN BRAID.

TAKE twenty-four strands, eighty hairs in a strand, and place on table like pattern. Commence at A, take Nos. 2 and lift across the table and lay between Nos. 2 at B, and bring back Nos. 2 from B to A; then change Nos. 1

the same way; then go to C, take Nos. 2 and lift them across the table and lay between Nos. 2 at D, and bring back Nos. 2 from D to A; then change Nos. 1 the same way; then go to E, take Nos. 1 and 2 and lift them across the table to F, and lay No. 1 from E at the right of No. 1 at F, and No. 2 from E at the right of No. 2 at F, and bring back the Nos. 1 and 2 from F to E; then go to G and change the same from G to H as you did at E and F. Then you are through the braid, ready to commence at A, as at first.

Braid this over a small wire, with a hole in one end like the eye of a needle, so as to draw a small cord in the place of the wire. When you have it braided, take off your weights, tie the ends fast on the wire, and push the braid together; then boil in water about ten minutes, and then take out and put it in an oven as hot as it will bear without burning, until it is quite dry; then take it out and slip it off the wire and on the cord, and sew the ends so it will not slip, and put a little shellac on the end to keep it fast. If you want it elastic, use elastic cord. To vary the size of the braid, vary the number of hairs in a strand.

FANCY TWIST BRAID.

TAKE twenty-four strands, seventy hairs in a strand, and place on table like pattern. Commence at A, take Nos. 1 cross over and lay between Nos. 1 at B, and bring back Nos. 2 from B and lay between Nos. 2 at A; then go to E, take Nos. 1 and 2 and cross over to F, and lay No. 1 down at the right of No. 1 at F, and No. 2 at the right of No. 2 at F, and and bring back Nos. 1 and 2 from F to E; then go to C, and change the Nos. at C and D the same as you did at A and B; then go to G, and change the Nos. at G and H the same as you did at E and F. Then you are through the braid, ready to commence at A, as at first.

Braid this over a small wire, with a hole in one end like the eye of a needle, so as to draw a small cord in the place of the wire. When you have it braided, take off your weights, tie the ends fast on the wire, and push the braid together; then boil in water about ten minutes, and then take out and put it in an oven as hot as it will bear without burning, until it is quite dry; then take it out and slip it off the wire and on the cord, and sew the ends so it will not slip, and put a little shellac on the end to keep it fast. If you want it elastic, use elastic cord. To vary the size of the braid vary the number of hairs in a strand.

FLAT CHAIN BRAID.

TAKE twenty-four strands, seventy hairs in a strand, and place on table like pattern. Commence at A, take Nos. 1 and change places by crossing one over the other; then go to B and cross the Nos. 1 the same way; then go back to A, take Nos. 1 and cross over and lay between Nos. 1 at B, and bring back Nos. 1 from B to A; then take Nos. 2 at A, and cross over and lay between Nos. 2 at B, and bring back Nos. 2 from B to A; then change Nos. 3 and 4 the same way; then go to C, take Nos. 1 and 2 and cross over to D, and lay the No. 1 from C down at the left of No. 1 at D, and the No. 2 from C down at the left of No. 2 at D, and bring back the Nos. 1 and 2 from D to C; then take the Nos. 3 and 4, cross over to D and lay the No. 3 from C down at the right of No. 3 at D, and the No. 4 from C down at the right of No. 4 at D, and bring back Nos. 3 and 4 from D to C. Then you are through the braid, ready to commence at A, as at first.

NECKLACE PATTERN.

TAKE sixteen strands, twenty hairs in a strand, and place on table like pattern. Commence at A, take Nos. 1 and 4 left across to B, lay in place of Nos. 1 and 4 at B, and bring back Nos. 1 and 4 from B to A; then take No. 2 at A in right hand and No. 3 in left hand, pass right hand round table to the right to B, and lay the No. 2 from A in place of No. 3 at B, and bring back No. 2 from B to A in right hand, and pass left hand round table to the left, and lay No. 3 from A in place of No. 2 at B, and bring back No. 3 from B to A, and lay No. 3 from B down at No. 2 at A, and lay No. 2 from B down at No. 3 at A, then go to C and take Nos. 1 across over inside of Nos. 1 at D, and bring back Nos. 1 from D to C; then go to A and repeat this all three times; then the fourth time at C you take Nos. 1 at C across over to D and lay outside of Nos. 2 at D, bring back the

Nos. 1 from D to C and lay them outside of Nos. 2 at C; then you are through the braid, ready to commence as at first at A. Braid it over a small cord so as to put it up together.

NECKLACE PATTERN.

TAKE sixteen strands, twenty hairs in a strand, and place on table like pattern. Commence at A, take Nos. 1 at A lift across inside of Nos. 1 at B, and bring back Nos. 1 from B to A; then go to C, take Nos. 1 at C lift across inside of Nos. 1 at D, and bring back Nos. 1 from D to C; then commence at A again and repeat it three times; then commence at A, take Nos. 1 across to B and lay them outside of Nos. 2 at B, and bring back Nos. 1 from B to A and lay outside of Nos. 2 at A; then go to C and change from C to D the same as from A to B; then you are through the braid, ready to commence as at first.

Braid this over a small wire, with a hole in one end like the eye of a needle, so as to draw a small cord in the place of the wire. When you have it braided, take off your weights, tie the ends fast on the wire and push the braid together on the wire; then boil in water about ten minutes; then take it out and put in an oven as hot as it will bear without burning, until it is quite dry; then take it out and slip it off of the wire on to the cord, and sew the ends of the braid so it will not slip on the cord, and put a little shellac on the end to keep it fast. If you want it elastic, use elastic cord. To vary the size of the braid, vary the number of hairs in a strand.

NECKLACE PATTERN.

TAKE sixteen strands, twenty hairs in a strand, and place on table like pattern. Commence at A, take Nos. 1 at A across over inside of Nos. 1 at B, and bring back Nos. 1 from B to A; then take Nos. 2 at A across over inside of Nos. 2 at B, and bring back Nos. 2 from B to A; then take No. 1 at C in right hand and No. 1 at D in left hand and change them, lay the No. 1 from C in place of No. 1 at D, and lay the No. 1 from D in place of No. 1 at C; then change the Nos. 1 and 2 at A and B as at first; then change the Nos. 2 at C and

D, as you did the Nos. 1 at C and D; then change the Nos. 1 and 2, as before, at A and B; then take Nos. 3 at C and D and change as you did the Nos. 2 at C and D; then change again Nos. 1 and 2 at A and B as at first; then take the Nos. 4 at C and D and change as you did the Nos. 3 at C and D; then you are through the braid, ready to commence as at first.

Braid this without cord or wire.

NECKLACE PATTERN.

TAKE sixteen strands, twenty hairs in a strand, and place on table like pattern. Commence at A, take Nos. 1 lift over to B in place of Nos. 1 at B, and bring back Nos. 1 from B to A; then take Nos. 2 at A and change over in place of Nos. 2 at B, and bring back Nos. 2 from B to A; then take No. 3 at A in right hand and No. 3 at B in left hand, and lay them inside of Nos. 1 at D, and bring back Nos. 1 from D and lay in place of Nos. 3 at A and B; then take No. 4 at A in left hand and No. 4 at B in right hand, and lay inside of Nos. 1 at C, and bring back Nos. 1 from C to A and B, and lay in place of Nos. 4; then commence as at first and repeat this three times, then take Nos. 1 at A, lift over to B in place of Nos. 1 at B, and bring back Nos. 1 from B to A; then take Nos. 2 at A and change over in place of Nos. 2 at B, and bring back Nos. 2 from B to A; then take Nos. 3 at A and B, lay inside of Nos. 1 at D; then take Nos. 4 at A and B, lay inside of Nos. 1 at C; then take Nos. 2 at A and lay outside of Nos. 1 at B, and bring back Nos. 2 from B and lay outside of Nos. 1 at A; then take Nos. 1 at C, lift over inside of Nos. 1 at D and bring back Nos. 1 from D and lay inside of Nos. 1 at C; then take No. 1 at C, on the side next to B, in right hand, and lay it inside of No. 1 at B; then take the No. 1 at D, next to B, in left hand, and lay it inside of No. 1 at B; then take the No. 1 at C, next to A, in right hand, and lay it inside of No. 1 at A; then take No. 1 at D, next to A, and lay it inside of No. 1 at A; then take the Nos. 3 and 4 at A, lift over to B, and lay outside of Nos. 1 at B, and bring back Nos. 3 and 4 from B and lay outside of Nos. 1 at A; then lift Nos. 2 at A over and lay in place of Nos. 2 at B, and bring back Nos. 2 from B to A, and lay in place of Nos. 2 at A; then take No. 4 at A, in left hand, and No. 4 at B in right hand, and lay them inside of

Nos. 1 at C, and bring the Nos. 1 from C back in place of the Nos. 4 at A and B; then take No. 3 at B in left hand, and No. 3 at A in right hand, and lay them inside of Nos. 1 at D, and bring back Nos. 1 from D and lay in place of Nos. 3 at A and B; then you are through the braid, ready to commence as at first.

NECKLACE PATTERN.

TAKE twenty-two strands, fifteen hairs in a strand, and place on table like pattern. Have the strands at A and B black hair, and those at C and D light hair. Commence at A, take Nos. 1 and cross over inside of Nos. 1 at B, and bring back Nos. 1 from B and lay in place of Nos. 1 at A, then take Nos. 2 at A, cross over inside of Nos. 2 at B, and bring back Nos. 2 from B and lay inside of Nos. 2 at A; then take No. 1 at C in right hand, and No. 1 at D in left hand, cross over and lay the No. 1 from C at D, and the No. 1 from D at C; then change the Nos. 1 and 2 at A and B as at first; then take the Nos. 2 at C and D and change them as you did the Nos. 1; then change again at A and B as at first; then take the Nos. 3 at C and D, and change as you did the Nos. 2; then change again at A and B, and so on till you get to Nos. 7, and after changing that, change again at A and B; then change Nos. 7 again, then those at A and B, then Nos. 6, then at A and B, then Nos. 5, and so on back to No. 1, and change No. 1 there as you did Nos. 7. Always braid those at A and B between each of those at C and D.

NECKLACE PATTERN.

TAKE 24 strands, twenty-five hairs in a strand, and place on table like this pattern. Commence at A, take Nos. 1 lift across inside of Nos. 1 at B, and bring back Nos. 1 from B to A, then go to C and take Nos. 1 at C and cross inside of Nos. 1 at D, and bring back Nos. 1 from D to C, then go to A and change Nos. 1 from A to B, as at first, then take Nos. 1 at E and F and swing round table with the same, and lay down in between Nos. 1 at A and B, and lay the No. 1 at A and B in the place of No. 4 at E and F, then change the Nos. 1 at C across inside of Nos. 1 at D, and bring back Nos. 1 from D to C, then change Nos. 1 at A and B the same, then the Nos. 1 at C and D again, then take Nos. 1 at H and G, swing round table with the same, and lay in between Nos. 1 at C and D, and lay the right hand ones at C and D up in place of No. 4 at H and G, then you are through the braid ready to commence as at first. Braid it over a cord so to push it together.

NECKLACE OR EDGING BRAID.

TAKE sixteen strands, fifteen hairs in a strand, and place on table like pattern. Commence at A, lift Nos. 2 across inside of Nos. 2 at B, and bring back Nos. 2 from B to A; then take Nos. 1 at A, lift across inside of Nos. 1 at B, and cross them, the one in right hand over the left, and bring back Nos. 1 from B to A, and cross the right over the left; then go to D, lift Nos. 1 across inside of Nos. 1 at C, cross the right over the left, and bring back Nos. 1 from C to D, and cross the right over the left; then repeat all from the beginning three times round the table. Then go to D, lift Nos. 3, cross the right over the left, and lay them outside of Nos. 1 at C; then go to A, lift Nos. 2 across inside of Nos. 2 at B, and bring back Nos. 2 from B to A; then take Nos. 1 at A, lift across inside of Nos. 1 at B, cross the right over the left, and bring back Nos. 1 from B to A, and cross them; then go to D, lift Nos. 1 across inside of Nos. 1 at C, cross the right over the left, and bring back Nos. 1 from C to D; then take Nos. 3 at C, and lay inside of Nos. 2 at D, and leave them there. Then you are through the braid, ready to commence at A, as at first.

HEAD DRESS OR NECKLACE BRAID.

TAKE twenty-four strands, eighty hairs in a strand, and place on table like pattern. Commence at A, lift Nos. 1 and 2 across inside of Nos. 1 and 2 at B, and bring back Nos. 1 and 2 from B to A; then go to C, lift Nos. 1 and 2 across inside of Nos. 1 and 2 at D, and bring back Nos. 1 and 2 from D to C; then go to A and change the Nos. 1 and 2 from A to B the same as at first; then take Nos. 1 at E and F, swing round table to the left, and lay them down between Nos. 1 and 2 at A and B; then lay the Nos. 2 at A and B in place of Nos. 4 at E and F; then change the Nos. 1 and 2 at C across inside of Nos. 1 and 2 at D, and bring back Nos. 1 and 2 from D to C; then change the same at A and B;

then change again at C and D the same; then take Nos. 1 at H and G, swing round table to the left, and lay them between Nos. 1 and 2 at C and D, and lay the Nos. 2 at C and D in place of Nos. 4 at H and G. Then you are through the braid, ready to commence at A, as at first.

Braid it over a strong cord, and when braided push it close together, tie the ends, and boil in water five minutes; then heat it in an oven until it is quite dry, and it is ready for use.

RING PATTERN.

TAKE thirteen strands, fifteen hairs in a strand, and place on table like pattern. Commence at A, lift No. 5 over between Nos. 2 and 3 at A; then take No. 1 at A, and lift over between Nos. 2 and 3 at B; then take No. 1 at B, and lift over between Nos. 2 and 3 at C; then lift No. 1 at C over between Nos. 2 and 3 at C; then lift No. 4 at C over between Nos. 2 and 3 at B; then lift No. 4 at B over between Nos. 2 and 3 at A. Then you are through the braid, ready to commence as at first, and repeating until it is the required length. Then tie it out straight on a flat stick, boil it in water five minutes, then heat it in an oven as hot as it will bear without burning, until it is quite dry, and then it is ready for use.

The above directions, after braiding, will suffice for finishing all Ring Braids, unless other directions are given.

RING BRAID.

TAKE twenty-four strands, twenty hairs in the strands at C and D, and ten hairs in the strands at A and B, and place on table like pattern. Commence at A, take Nos. 1 and lift across table and lay inside of Nos. 1 at B, and bring back Nos. 2 from B and lay outside of Nos. 2 at A; then go to C, take Nos. 1, cross over and lay in between Nos. 1 at D, and bring back Nos. 1 from D to C; then take Nos. 3 at C, cross inside of Nos. 3 at D, and bring back Nos. 3 from D to C; then take Nos. 4 at C, cross over inside of Nos. 4 at D, and bring back Nos. 4

from D to C; then commence at A, and change them at A and B as at first; then go to C and commence with the Nos. 2. You must leave the Nos. 1 every other time and the Nos. 2 every other time, and braid it as at first.

RIB RING BRAID.

TAKE nineteen strands, twenty hairs in a strand, and place on table like pattern. Commence at A, take No. 1 and lift over Nos. 2 and 3, under 4 and 5, over 6, 7, 8, 9 and 10, and lay over to B; then take No. 1 at B, lift over Nos. 2 and 3, under 4 and 5, over 6, 7, 8, 9 and 10, and lay over to A; then you are through the braid, ready to commence at A, as at first,--first round to the left, and then to the right, and so on, repeating the changes as above, until the braid is finished. Then tie it out straight on a flat stick, boil in water five minutes, then heat it in an oven as hot as it will bear without burning until it is quite dry, and then it is ready for use.

RING PATTERN.

TAKE twenty strands, twenty hairs in a strand, and place on table like pattern. Commence at A, take the Nos. 1 and lift across the table and lay in place of Nos. 1 at B, and bring back Nos. 1 from B to A; then take the Nos. 2, 3 and 4, and change the same; then go to C, take the Nos. 1 and lift across the table and lay in place of Nos. 1 at D, and bring back Nos. 1 from D to C; then commence again at A, take Nos. 1 and lift over the table and lay in the place of Nos. 1 at B, and bring back the Nos. 1 from B to A; then change the Nos. 2 and 3 the same as the Nos. 1; then go to C and change the Nos. 1 over in the place of Nos. 1 at D, and bring back the Nos. 1 from D to C; then go to A, and take the Nos. 1, 2 and 3, and change the same as before; then go to C and change the same as before. Then you are through the braid ready to commence at A, as at first, and repeat until the braid is finished.

RING PATTERN.

TAKE twenty strands, twenty hairs in a strand, and place on table like pattern. Commence at A, take Nos. 1 and lift over across the table, and lay in place of Nos. 1 at B, and bring back Nos. 1 from B and lay in place of Nos. 1 at A; then take Nos. 2, 3 and 4, and change their places the same as Nos. 1; then go to C, take Nos. 1 and lift over across the table and lay in place of Nos. 1 at D, and bring back Nos. 1 from D to C; then go to A, take Nos. 1 and lift them over the table and lay in place of Nos. 1 at B, and bring back Nos. 1 from B to A; then take Nos. 3 and 4 and change the same; then go to C, take Nos. 1 and lift them over the table and lay in place of Nos. 1 at D, and bring back Nos. 1 from D to C. Then you are through the braid, ready to commence at A, as at first, and repeat the changes until the braid is finished.

RING PATTERN.

TAKE twenty strands, fifteen hairs in a strand, and place on table like pattern. Commence at A, take Nos. 1, lift across to B, and lay inside of Nos. 1, and bring back Nos. 2 from B and lay in between Nos. 2 at A; then go to C, take Nos. 1 and lift over inside of Nos. 1 at D, and bring back Nos. 1 from D to C; then take Nos. 2 at C, and cross over inside of Nos. 2 at D, and bring back Nos. 2 from D to C; then take Nos. 3 at C, cross over inside of Nos. 3 at D, and bring back Nos. 3 from D to C; then commence again at A, as at first, and repeat until it is braided the desired length.

When the braid is finished, tie it out straight on a flat stick, boil in water five minutes, and heat in an oven until perfectly dry, and then it is ready for use.

RING PATTERN.

TAKE twenty strands, twenty hairs in a strand, and lay on table like pattern. Commence at A, take Nos. 1 and lift over table and lay in place of Nos. 1 at B, and bring back Nos. 1 from B to A; then take Nos. 2 and change the same; then the Nos. 3, and change the same; then go to C, take the Nos. 2 and lay outside of the Nos. 1; then go to D, and take the Nos. 2 and lay outside of the Nos. 1; then go to C, and take Nos. 2 and lift over table and lay in place of Nos. 2 at D, and bring back the Nos. 2 from D to C; then go to A, take Nos. 1 and lift across the table and lay in place of Nos. 1 at B, and bring back Nos. 1 from B to A; then take Nos. 3 at A, and lift across table in place of Nos. 3 at B, and bring back Nos. 3 from B to A; then go to C, take Nos. 2 and lay outside of Nos. 1; then go to D, take Nos. 2 and lay outside of Nos. 1; then go to C, take Nos. 2 and lift over table in place of Nos. 2 at D, and bring back Nos. 2 from D to C. Then you are ready to commence at A, as at first, and repeat until finished.

RING PATTERN.

TAKE fifteen strands, twenty hairs in a strand, and place on table like pattern. Commence at A, by taking No. 1 and lifting it over Nos. 2, 3 and 4, under Nos. 5, 6, 7 and 8, and pass it over to B; then take No. 1 at B, lift over Nos. 2, 3 and 4, under 5, 6, 7 and 8, and pass it over to A; then you are through, ready to commence at A, as at first, and repeat until the braid is finished,--first round to the left, and then round to the right.

RING PATTERN.

TAKE nineteen strands, ten hairs in a strand, and place on table like pattern. Commence at A, take No. 1 and lift over Nos. 2, 3 and 4, under 5 and 6, over 7 and 8, under 9 and 10, and pass it over to B; then take No. 1 at B, and lift over Nos. 2, 3 and 4, under 5 and 6, over 7 and 8, under 9 and 10, and lay it over to A; then go to A and commence at No. 1, as at first, and repeat over and over, first to the left and then to the right, and so on, until the braid is finished. Then tie it out straight on a flat stick, boil in water five minutes, and heat it in an oven as hot as it will bear without burning, until it is quite dry, and then it is ready for use.

RING PATTERN.

TAKE twenty-four strands, and place on table like pattern. Commence at A, take Nos. 1 and lift across inside of Nos. 1 at B, and bring back Nos. 2 inside of Nos. 2 at A; then go to C, and take Nos. 1 and cross over inside of Nos. 1 at D, and bring back Nos. 1 from D to C; then take Nos. 2 at C, and cross over inside of Nos. 2 at D, and bring back Nos. 2 from D to C; then take Nos. 3 at C, and cross over inside of Nos. 3 at D, and bring back Nos. 3 from D to C; then take Nos. 4 at C, and cross over inside of Nos. 4 at D, and bring back Nos. 4 from D to C; if you wish to reverse every other time, you may leave the Nos. 1 and not braid them; then you are ready to commence at A as at first.

RING PATTERN.

TAKE twenty-four strands, sixteen hairs in a strand, and place on the table like pattern. Commence at A, take Nos. 1 and cross over to B, lay in between Nos. 1 at B, and bring back Nos. 1 from B and lay in place of Nos. 1 at A; then take Nos. 2 at A, and change them the same way; then Nos. 3 the same; then Nos. 4 the same. Then take Nos. 1 at C and D, and lift over Nos. 2; then lift Nos. 1 at C over in place of Nos. 1 at D, and bring back Nos. 1 from D to C; then go to A, and take Nos. 2, cross over between Nos. 2 at B, and bring back Nos. 2 from B to A; then take Nos. 3 and change the same way; then take Nos. 4 and change the same. Then go to C and D, and lift Nos. 1 over Nos. 2, and then lift Nos. 1 at C over and lay in place of Nos. 1 at D, and bring back Nos. 1 from D and lay in place of Nos. 1 at C; then you are ready to commence as at first, at A, and repeat until the braid is finished. You will place double weight on the strands at C and D.

RING PATTERN.

TAKE twenty-eight strands, of twelve hairs, and place on table like pattern. Commence at A, take Nos. 1 and cross over the table and lay in place of Nos. 1 at B, and bring back Nos. 1 from B to A; then change the Nos. 2 the same. Then take Nos. 4 at A, and lift over the table in place of Nos. 4 at B, and bring back Nos. 4 from B to A; then take Nos. 5 and change the same way. Then go to C and D, and lift the Nos. 1 over the Nos. 2; then take Nos. 1 at C, and lift them over the table inside of Nos. 1 at D, and bring back the Nos. 1 from D and lay in place of Nos. 1 at C; then go to A, and take Nos. 1 and cross over in place of Nos. 1 at B, and bring back Nos. 1 from B to A; then take Nos. 2, 3, 4 and 5, and change all the same. Then go to C and D, and lift Nos. 1 over Nos. 2;

then lift Nos. 1 at C over the table, and lay them inside of Nos. 1 at D, and bring back Nos. 1 from D to C. Then you are through the braid, ready to commence at A, as at first, and repeat until the braid is finished. Place extra weight on the strands at C and D.

RING OR BRACELET PATTERN.

TAKE twenty-four strands, twenty hairs in a strand, and place on table like pattern, thirteen on the right side and eleven on the left. Take No. 1 at right hand, lift over Nos. 2 3 and 4, and under Nos. 5 and 6, and over No. 7; then take No. 1 again, in right hand, and lift over Nos. 2 3 and 4, and under Nos. 5 and 6; then take the same two that you have braided along, and lift over two strands, and under two, till you get to the center; then pass the same two strands across to the left side, and lay them down next to No. 11; then commence on the left side with No. 1, and braid the left side as you did the right; then the braid is through, ready to commence as at first, with No. 1 at right hand, and so on. Repeat till finished.

RING PATTERN.

TAKE thirteen strands, twelve hairs in a strand, and place on table like pattern. Commence by lifting No. 7 over Nos. 6 and 5, and under Nos. 4 and 3, and over Nos. 2 and 1, and lay it next to No. 1 on the left side, making seven on the left side; then commence on the left side, take the outside one and braid it into the middle, over two and under two, till you get to the center, and lay it across on the opposite side; then you are through with the braid, and ready to commence as at first, with the No. 7 at right hand. You can have any odd number of strands you please.

RING PATTERN.

TAKE twenty strands, ten hairs in a strand, and lay on table like pattern. Commence at A, take No. 2 in right hand and swing it round the table to the right, and lay it across No. 2 at B, and bring back No. 2 from B to A; then take

No. 1 at A in left hand, and swing it round the table to the left, and lay it across No. 1 at B, and bring back No. 1 from B to A. Then commence at C and D; take No. 1 at C in left hand, and No. 1 at D in right hand, and change places with them by passing the left hand over the right; then take Nos. 2 at C and D, and change the same way; then take Nos. 3 and change the same way; then take Nos. 4 and change the same way. Then go to B, and change the Nos. 1 at E and F as you did at C and D, by commencing at Nos. 1 first, then the Nos. 2, 3 and 4, in succession. Then you are through the braid, ready to commence as at first, at A. Braid it over a small wire.

BRACELET TIGHT BRAID.

TAKE any number of strands that can be divided by four,--sixty being the usual number--fifteen hairs in a strand, and place on table like pattern. Commence at A, with the inside row of figures, lift No. 3 over No. 2, and Nos. 1 and 3 over Nos. 2 and 4, and so on round table to the left, till you get to A; then go to C, braid to the left, lift Nos. 1 and 2 over Nos. 3 and 4, and so on round to A; then commence at A and braid round to the right; lift No. 2 over No. 3, and Nos. 3 and 4 over Nos. 2 and 1, and so on round table to A; then go to C, braid round to the right, and lift Nos. 2 and 4 over Nos. 3 and 1, and so on round to A. Then you are through the braid, ready to commence as at first.

Braid this over a round stick, the size you want the braid for use, varying the number of strands according to the size of the stick; then slip the braid from the stick on to the mold you wish to use, tying it so it will fit the mold exactly, and then boil in water five minutes, and take it out and put it in an oven as hot as it will bear without burning, until it is quite dry. Then it is ready for use.

BRACELET BRAID.

TAKE sixteen strands, thirty hairs in a strand, and place on the table like pattern. Commence at A, take the Nos. 1 and 2 and lay them over Nos. 3 right and left; then lay the Nos. 1 at A over Nos. 1 at C and D, and bring back the Nos. 1 from C and D and lay outside of Nos. 3 at A; then lay the Nos. 2 at A over Nos. 1; then go to B and repeat the same as at A, only change the Nos. 1 at B with the Nos. 2 at C, instead of the Nos. 1 at C; then lift the Nos. 1 at A over and lay between Nos. 1 at B, and bring back Nos. 1 from B to A; then go to C and lift Nos. 1 and 2 over between Nos. 1 and 2 at D, and bring back the Nos. 1 and 2 from D to C. Then you are through the braid, ready to commence at A, as at first. Braid this over a small wire, and place double weight on the strands at C and D, and Nos. 1 at A and B.

BRACELET BRAID.

TAKE any number of strands that can be divided by four,--forty being the usual number for this braid--twelve hairs in a strand, and place on table like pattern. Commence at A, with the inside row of figures, and lift No. 3 over No. 2; then No. 1 over No. 2; then No. 4 over Nos. 3 and 2; then go to B and change the same way, and so on round the table to A. Then go to C, commence with the outside row of figures, and braid round to the left; lift No. 2 over No. 3; then No. 3 over No. 4; then No. 2 over No. 1; then No. 2 over No. 3, and so on round the table to A; then you will be through the braid, ready to commence as at first.

Braid this over a round stick, the size you want the braid for use, varying the number of strands according to the size of the stick; then slip the braid from the stick on to the mold you wish to use, tying the braid so it will fit the mold exactly, and then boil in water five minutes, and take it out and put it in an oven, as hot as it will bear without burning, until it is quite dry. Then it is ready for use.

ELASTIC BRACELET BRAID.

TAKE any number of strands that can be divided by four,--forty being the usual number for this braid--fifteen hairs in a strand, and place on table like pattern. Commence at A, with the inside row of figures, lift No. 2 in right hand, and put your left hand under the right hand, and take Nos. 3 and 4 and bring them back, and cross them over No. 1, and lay them all down; then go to B, and change the same way, and so on round the table to A. Then go to C, commence with the outside row of figures, and braid round to the left; lift No. 3 in left hand, and put your right hand under the left hand and take Nos. 1 and 2, bring them back, cross them over No. 4, and lay them all down, and so on round the table to A; then you will be through the braid, ready to commence as at first.

Braid this over a round stick, the size you want the braid for use, varying the number of strands according to the size of the stick; then slip the braid from the stick on to the mold you wish to use, tying the braid so it will fit the mold exactly, and then boil in water five minutes, and take it out and put it in an oven, as hot as it will bear without burning, until it is quite dry. Then it is ready for use.

ELASTIC BRACELET BRAID.

TAKE any number of strands that can be divided by four--sixty being the usual number for this braid--fifteen hairs in a strand, and place on table like pattern. Commence at A, with the inside row of figures, and braid round table to the right; lift No. 1 over No. 2, and No. 4 over Nos. 3 and 2; then repeat with the same strands, the No. 1 over No. 2, and No. 4 over Nos. 3 and 2. Then go to B and braid the same, and so on round table to A. Then go to C, commence with the outside row of figures, and braid round table to the left; lift No. 1 over No. 2, and No. 4 over Nos. 3 and 2; then repeat with the same strands, the same as you did at A and B, and so on round table to A. Then you are through the braid, ready to commence as at first. After it is braided turn the braid inside out.

Braid this over a round stick, the size you want the braid for use, varying the number of strands according to the size of the stick; then slip the braid from the stick on to the mold you wish to use, and push it tight together, tying it so it will fit the mold exactly, and then boil in water five minutes, and take it out and put it in an oven as hot as it will bear without burning, until it is quite dry. Then it is ready for use.

DOUBLE ELASTIC BRACELET BRAID.

TAKE any number of strands that can be divided by four--sixty being the usual number for this braid--fifteen hairs in a strand, and place on table like pattern. Commence at A, with the inside row of figures; and braid round table to the right; cross No. 4 over No. 3, and No. 1 over Nos. 2 and 3; then repeat with the same strands. Then go to B, and braid the same, and so on round table to the right, until you get to A. Then go to C, and braid back round table to the left, by crossing No. 2 over No. 1, and No. 3 over No. 4, and No. 2 over No. 3; then repeat with the same strands, and so on round table till you get to A. Then you are through the braid, ready to commence as at first.

Braid this over a round stick, the size you want the braid for use, varying the number of strands according to the size of the stick; then slip the braid from the stick on to the mold you wish to use, and push it tight together, tying it so it will fit the mold exactly, and then boil in water five minutes, and take it out and put it in an oven as hot as it will bear without burning, until it is quite dry. Then it is ready for use.

FANCY TIGHT BRACELET BRAID.

TAKE any number of strands that can be divided by four,--sixty being the usual number--fifteen hairs in a strand, and place on table like pattern. Commence at A, with the inside row of figures, lift No. 3 over No. 2, and Nos. 1 and 3 over Nos. 2 and 4; then go to B, and braid the same to the left until you get to A; then commence at C, with the outside row of figures, and braid round table to the left again; lift Nos. 1 and 2 over Nos. 3 and 4, and so on round table till you get to A. Then commence with the inside row of figures at A, and lift No. 2 over No. 3, and Nos. 2 and 4 over Nos. 3 and 1; then go to B, and braid the same to the right, and so on round table to A; then commence at C with the outside row of figures, and braid round to the right, lift Nos. 3 and 4 over Nos. 2 and 1, and so on round table to A; then you are through the braid, ready to commence as at first. Be sure and braid the first two times round table to the left, and the last two to the right.

Braid this over a round stick, the size you want the braid for use, varying the number of strands according to the size of the stick; then slip the braid from the stick on to the mold you wish to use, tying it so it will fit the mold exactly, and then boil in water five minutes, and take it out and put it in an oven as hot as it will bear without burning, until it is quite dry. Then it is ready for use. To have it elastic use elastic cord.

REVERSE TIGHT BRACELET BRAID.

TAKE any number of strands that can be divided by four,--sixty being the usual number--fifteen hairs in a strand, and place on table like pattern. Commence at A, with the inside row of figures, lift No. 3 over No. 2, and No. 1 over No. 2, then No. 4 over Nos. 3 and 2; then go to B and change the same to the left, and so on round table to A; then go to C, braid to the left with the outside row of figures, lift Nos. 3 and 4 over Nos. 1 and 2, and so on round to A. Then commence again at A and braid round to the right; lift No. 2 over No. 3, then No. 2 over No. 1, and Nos. 2 and 3 over No. 4, and so on round table to A; then commence at C and braid to the right, lift Nos. 1 and 2 over Nos. 3 and 4, and so on round to A. Then you are through the braid, ready to commence as at first.

Braid this over a round stick, the size you want the braid for use, varying the number of strands according to the size of the stick; then slip the braid from the stick on to the mold you wish to use, tying it so it will fit the mold exactly, and then boil in water five minutes, and take it out and put it in an oven as hot as it will bear without burning, until it is quite dry. Then it is ready for use.

BANDED BRACELET BRAID.

TAKE any number of strands that can be divided by four,--sixty being the usual number--fifteen hairs in a strand, and place on table like pattern. Commence at A, with the inside row of figures, lift No. 3 over No. 2, and No. 1

over No. 2, then No. 3 over No. 4, and No. 3 over No. 2; braid round table to the left till you get to A, then repeat the same at C with the outside row of figures. After braiding the second time round, commence again at A, with the inside row of figures, and braid round to the right; lift Nos. 3 and 4 over Nos. 1 and 2, and so on round to A; then repeat, at C, with the outside row of figures. Then you are through the braid, ready to commence as at first.

Braid this over a round stick, the size you want the braid for use, varying the number of strands according to the size of the stick; then slip the braid from the stick on to the mold you wish to use, tying it so it will fit the mold exactly, and then boil in water five minutes, and take it out and put it in an oven as hot as it will bear without burning, until it is quite dry. Then it is ready for use.

PLAIN OPEN BRAID.

TAKE any number of strands that can be divided by four,--sixty being the usual number--fifteen hairs in a strand, and place on table like pattern. Commence at A, with the inside row of figures, lift No. 1 over No. 2, No. 4 over No. 3, No. 1 over No. 2, and No. 4 over No. 3; then No. 3 over No. 2, No. 1 over No. 2, and No. 4 over Nos. 2 and 3. Braid round table to the left till you get to A, then repeat the same at C, only braid the outside row of figures. Then you are through the braid, ready to commence as at first.

Braid this over a round stick, the size you want the braid for use, varying the number of strands according to the size of the stick; then slip the braid from the stick on to the mold you wish to use, tying it so it will fit the mold exactly, and then boil in water five minutes, and take it out and put it in an oven as hot as it will bear without burning, until it is quite dry. Then it is ready for use.

OPEN FINE BRAID.

TAKE any number of strands that can be divided by four,--eighty being The usual number for this braid--four hairs in a strand, and place on table like pattern. Commence at A, with the inside row of figures, lift No. 2 over No. 3;

then No. 2 over No. 1; then No. 2 over No. 3; then Nos. 2 and 3 over No. 4; then No. 2 over No. 1. Then go to B and change the same way, and so on round the table to A. Then go to C, and commence with the outside row of figures, and change the same as you did at A, and so on round the table, when you will be through the braid, ready to commence at A, as at first.

Braid this over a round stick, the size you want the braid for use, varying the number of strands according to the size of the stick; then slip the braid from the stick on to the mold you wish to use, tying the braid so it will fit the mold exactly, and then boil in water five minutes, and take it out and put it in an oven, as hot as it will bear without burning, until it is quite dry. Then it is ready for use.

OPEN FINE BRAID.

TAKE any number of Strands that can be divided by four,--eighty being the usual number for this braid--four hairs in a strand, and place on table like pattern. Commence at A, with the inside row of figures, lift No. 1 over Nos. 2, 3 and 4; then No. 3 over Nos. 2 and 1; then No. 2 over Nos. 3 and 4; then No. 2 over No. 1. Then go to B and change the same, and so on round the table to A. Then go to C, and commence with the outside row of figures, and change the same as you did at A, and so on round the table, when you will be through the braid, ready to commence at A, as at first.

Braid this over a round stick, the size you want the braid for use, varying the number of strands according to the size of the stick; then slip the braid from the stick on to the mold you wish to use, tying the braid so it will fit the mold exactly, and then boil in water five minutes, and take it out and put it in an oven, as hot as it will bear without burning, until it is quite dry. Then it is ready for use.

OPEN LACE BRAID.

TAKE any number of strands that can be divided by four,--sixty being the usual number--fifteen hairs in a strand, and place on table like pattern. Commence at A, with the inside row of figures, lift No. 3 over No. 2, No. 3 over No. 4, No. 1 over No. 2, No. 3 over No. 2, and so on round the table to the left to A; then commence at C, lift No. 3 over No. 2, No. 3 over No. 4, No. 1 over No. 2, No. 3 over No. 2, No. 1 over No. 2 and No. 3 over No. 4. Then you are through the braid, ready to commence as at first.

Braid this over a round stick, the size you want the braid for use, varying the number of strands according to the size of the stick; then slip the braid from the stick on to the mold you wish to use, tying it so it will fit the mold exactly, and then boil in water five minutes, and take it out and put it in an oven as hot as it will bear without burning, until it is quite dry. Then it is ready for use.

OPEN BRAID.

TAKE any number of strands that can be divided by four,--eighty being the usual number for this braid--four hairs in a strand, and place on table like pattern. Commence at A, with the inside row of figures, lift No. 3 over No. 2; then No. 3 over No 4; then No. 1 over No. 2; then No. 3 over No. 2; then No. 1 over No. 2; then No. 3 over No. 4. Then go to B and change the same way, and so on round the table to A. Then go to C, and commence with the outside row of figures, and change the same as you did at A, and so on round the table, when you will be through the braid, ready to commence at A, as at first.

Braid this over a round stick, the size you want the braid for use, varying the number of strands according to the size of the stick; then slip the braid from the stick on to the mold you wish to use, tying the braid so it will fit the mold exactly, and then boil in water five minutes, and take it out and put it in an oven, as hot as it will bear without burning, until it is quite dry. Then it is ready for use.

BASKET TIGHT BRAID.

TAKE thirty-two strands, or any number that can be divided by four, fifteen hairs in a strand, and place on table like pattern. Commence at A, with the inside row of figures, and braid round the table to the left; lift No. 3 over No. 2, No. 1 over No. 2, and No. 3 over No. 4; then commence at C, with the outside row of figures, and braid round the table to the left; lift Nos. 1 and 2 over Nos. 3 and 4; then commence at A, as before, and braid round the table to the right; put No. 3 under No. 2, and lift No. 2 over No. 1, and No. 3 over No. 4; then commence at C, as before, and braid round the table to the right, and put Nos. 1 and 2 under Nos. 3 and 4. Then you are through the braid, ready to commence at A, as at first.

Braid this over a round stick, the size you want the braid for use, varying the number of strands according to the size of the stick; then slip the braid from the stick on to the mold you wish to use, tying the braid so it will fit the mold exactly, and then boil in water five minutes, and take it out and put it in an oven, as hot as it will bear without burning, until it is quite dry. Then it is ready for use.

TIGHT BRAID.

TAKE any number of strands that can be divided by four,--forty being the usual number--twelve hairs in a strand, and place on table like pattern. Commence at A, with the inside row of figures, and lift Nos. 1 and 2 over Nos. 3 and 4; then go to B and change the same way, and so on round table to A. Then go to C, commence with the outside row of figures, and braid round to the left; lift Nos. 3 and 4 over Nos. 1 and 2, and so on round the table to A. Then you will be through the braid, ready to commence as at first.

Braid this over a round stick, the size you want the braid for use, varying the number of strands according to the size of the stick; then slip the braid from the stick on to the mold you wish to use, tying it so it will fit the mold exactly, and then boil in water five minutes, and take it out and put it in an oven as hot as it will bear without burning, until it is quite dry. Then it is ready for use.

ACORN TIGHT BRAID.

TAKE any number of strands that can be divided by four,--sixty being the usual number--fifteen hairs in a strand, and place on table like pattern. Commence at A, with the inside row of figures, lift No. 2 over No. 3, No. 4 over No. 3, No. 1 over No. 2, and No. 3 over No. 2, and so on round table to the right till you get to A; then commence at C, braid round to the right, lift Nos. 3 and 4 over Nos. 1 and 2, and so on round table to A. Then you are through the braid, ready to commence at A, as at first.

Braid this over a round stick, the size you want the braid for use, varying the number of strands according to the size of the stick; then slip the braid from the stick on to the mold you wish to use, tying it so it will fit the mold exactly, and then boil in water five minutes, and take it out and put it in an oven as hot as it will bear without burning, until it is quite dry. Then it is ready for use.

HALF TIGHT BRAID.

TAKE any number of strands that can be divided by four,--sixty being the usual number--fifteen hairs in a strand, and place on table like pattern. Commence at A, with the inside row of figures, lift No. 3 over No. 2, and Nos. 1 and 3 over Nos. 2 and 4, and so on round table to A; then commence at C with the outside row of figures, lift No. 2 over No. 3, No. 2 over No. 1, No. 2 over No. 3, Nos. 2 and 3 over No. 4, and No. 2 over No. 1, and so on round table to A. Then you are through the braid, ready to commence at A, as at first.

Braid this over a round stick, the size you want the braid for use, varying the number of strands according to the size of the stick; then slip the braid from the stick on to the mold you wish to use, tying it so it will fit the mold exactly, and then boil in water five minutes, and take it out and put it in an oven as hot as it will bear without burning, until it is quite dry. Then it is ready for use.

FANCY TIGHT BRAID.

IN this pattern you braid with eight strands, or with two groups of fours. Commence at B, lift No. 4 in left hand and lay down between Nos. 3 and 4 at C, and take No. 4 at C in right hand; then lift No. 3 at B over between Nos. 2 and 3 at C, and take No. 3 at C in right hand; then lift No. 2 at B over between Nos. 1 and 2 at C, and take No. 2 at C in right hand; then lift No. 1 at B over next to No. 1 at C, and take No. 1 at C in right hand, and then lift those in right hand over to B, and lay them all down. Braid round to the right till you get to A, then take the next eight strands, and braid round table to the left; lift No. 1 at C over between Nos. 1 and 2 at B, and take No. 1 at B in left hand; then lift No. 2 at C over between Nos. 2 and 3 at B, and take No. 2 at B in left hand; then lift No. 3 at C over between Nos. 3 and 4 at B, and take No. 3 at B in left hand; then lift No. 4 at C over next to No. 4 at B, and take No. 4 at B in left hand, and then lift those in left hand over to C and lay them all down, and so on round table, taking the next eight strands, till you get to A. Then you are through the braid, ready to commence as at first.

PLAIN TIGHT BRAID.

TAKE any number of strands that can be divided by four,--eighty being the usual number for this braid--four hairs in a strand, and place on table like pattern. Commence at A, with the inside row of figures, lift No. 3 over No. 2; then No. 3 over No. 4; then No. 1 over No. 2; then No. 3 over No. 2. Then go to B and change the same way, and so round the table to A. Then go to C, and commence with the outside row of figures, and change the same as you did at A, and so on round the table, when you will be through the braid, ready to commence at A, as at first.

Braid this over a round stick, the size you want the braid for use, varying the number of strands according to the size of the stick; then slip the braid from the stick on to the mold you wish to use, tying it so it will fit the mold exactly, and then boil in water five minutes, and take it out and put it in an oven as hot as it will bear without burning, until it is quite dry. Then it is ready for use.

ACORN BRAID.

TAKE any number of strands that can be divided by four,--sixty being the usual number--fifteen hairs in a strand, and place on table like pattern. Commence at A, with the inside row of figures, lift No. 3 over No. 2, No. 3 over No. 4, No. 1 over No. 2, and No. 3 over No. 2, and so on round table to A; then go to C, take the outside row of figures, and make the same changes round to A, and repeat alternately at A and C, until the braid is long enough to cover the bottom of the acorn, and then commence at A with the inside row of figures; lift No. 3 over No. 2, No. 3 over No. 4, No. 1 over No. 2, No. 3 over No. 2, No. 1 over No. 2, and No. 3 over No. 4, and so on round to A; then go to C, take the outside row of figures, and make the same changes round to A; then repeat until the braid is long enough to make the top or bur of the acorn. Then you are through the braid, ready to commence as at first.

Braid this over a round stick, the size you want the braid for use, varying the number of strands according to the size of the stick; then slip the braid from the stick on to the mold you wish to use, tying it so it will fit the mold exactly, and then boil in water five minutes, and take it out and put it in an oven as hot as it will bear without burning, until it is quite dry. Then it is ready for use.

HALF OPEN BRAID.

TAKE any number of strands that can be divided by four,--sixty being the usual number--fifteen hairs in a strand, and place on table like pattern. Commence at A, with the inside row of figures, lift No. 1 over between Nos. 2 and 3 at B; then lift No. 1 at B over between Nos. 2 and 3 of the next four strands, and so on round table to the left to A; then go to C, take the outside row of figures, lift No. 2 over No. 3, No. 2 over No. 1, Nos. 2 and 3 over No. 4; then No. 3 over No. 4, and No. 2 over No. 1, and so on round the table to the right, till the braid is finished.

Braid this over a round stick, the size you want the braid for use, varying the number of strands according to the size of the stick; then slip the braid from the stick on to the mold you wish to use, tying it so it will fit the mold exactly, and then boil in water five minutes, and take it out and put it in an oven as hot as it will bear without burning, until it is quite dry. Then it is ready for use.

OVERSHOT BRAID.

TAKE any number of strands that can be divided by four,--sixty being the usual number--fifteen hairs in a strand, and place on table like pattern. Commence at A, with the inside row of figures, braid to the right, lift No. 2 over Nos. 3 and 4, No. 1 over No. 2, and No. 3 over No. 2, and so on round to A; then go to C and repeat the same changes, with the outside row of figures, round to A; then commence at A with the inside row of figures, and braid to the left; lift No. 3 over Nos. 1 and 2, No. 4 over No. 3, and No. 2 over No. 3, and so on round to A; then go to C, and repeat the same changes, with the outside row of figures, round to A. Then you are through the braid, ready to commence as at first.

Braid this over a round stick, the size you want the braid for use, varying the number of strands according to the size of the stick; then slip the braid from the stick on to the mold you wish to use, tying it so it will fit the mold exactly, and then boil in water five minutes, and take it out and put it in an oven as hot as it will bear without burning, until it is quite dry. Then it is ready for use.

DIAMOND TIGHT BRAID.

TAKE any number of strands that can be divided by four,--sixty being the usual number--fifteen hairs in a strand, and place on table like pattern. Commence at A, with the inside row of figures, and have Nos. 1 and 2 of white hair, and Nos. 3 and 4 of black hair; lift Nos. 1 and 2 over Nos. 3 and 4, and so on round table to the left, to A; then go to C, and braid round table to the right; lift Nos. 3 and 4 over Nos. 1 and 2, and so on round table to A. Then you are through the braid, ready to commence as at first.

Braid this over a round stick, the size you want the braid for use, varying the number of strands according to the size of the stick; then slip the braid from the stick on to the mold you wish to use, tying it so it will fit the mold exactly, and then boil in water five minutes, and take it out and put it in an oven as hot as it will bear without burning, until it is quite dry. Then it is ready for use.

SPIRAL STRIPED BRAID.

TAKE any number of strands that can be divided by four,--sixty being the usual number--fifteen hairs in a strand, and place on table like pattern. Commence at A, with the inside row of figures, and have alternately four strands of white hair and four of black; braid round table to the left, lift Nos. 1 and 2 over Nos. 3 and 4, and so on round table to A; then go to C, braid round table to the right, lift Nos. 3 and 4 over Nos. 1 and 2, and so on round to A. Then you are through the braid, ready to commence as at first.

Braid this over a round stick, the size you want the braid for use, varying the number of strands according to the size of the stick; then slip the braid from the stick on to the mold you wish to use, tying it so it will fit the mold exactly, and then boil in water five minutes, and take it out and put it in an oven as hot as it will bear without burning, until it is quite dry. Then it is ready for use.

EMPRESS TIGHT BRAID.

TAKE any number of strands that can be divided by four,--sixty being the usual number--fifteen hairs in a strand, and place on table like pattern. Commence at A, with the inside row of figures, lift No. 3 over No. 2, No. 1 over No. 2, No. 3 over No. 4, and No. 3 over No. 2; braid round table to the left till you get to A, then go to C, take the outside row of figures, and braid round to the right; lift Nos. 3 and 4 over Nos. 1 and 2, and so on round to A, and repeat with the inside row of figures, and then repeat again with the outside row; then you are through the braid, ready to commence at A, as at first. Commence at C every other time, for you only braid the first change of figures once, and the last change three times.

Braid this over a round stick, the size you want the braid for use, varying the number of strands according to the size of the stick; then slip the braid from the stick on to the mold you wish to use, tying it so it will fit the mold exactly, and then boil in water five minutes, and take it out and put it in an oven as hot as it will bear without burning, until it is quite dry. Then it is ready for use.

OPEN CHECK BRAID.

TAKE any number of strands that can be divided by four,--eighty being the usual number--four hairs in a strand, and place on table like pattern. Have one-half the strands white and one-half black, and place on table alternately, four white and four black. Commence at A, with the inside row of figures, lift No. 2 over No. 3, No. 2 over No. 1, No. 2 over No. 3, Nos. 2 and 3 over No. 4, and No. 2 over No. 1. Then go to B and change the same way, and so on round table to A. Then go to C, commence with the outside row of figures, and change the same as you did at A, and so on round the table; then you will be through the braid, ready to commence at A, as at first.

Braid this over a round stick, the size you want the braid for use, varying the number of strands according to the size of the stick; then slip the braid from the stick on to the mold you wish to use, tying it so it will fit the mold exactly, and then boil in water five minutes, and take it out and put it in an oven as hot as it will bear without burning, until it is quite dry. Then it is ready for use.

SCOTCH PLAID BRAID.

TAKE any number of strands that can be divided by four,--eighty being the usual number--four hairs in a strand, and place on table like pattern. Have one-third the strands white hair, one-third black, and one-third red, and place on table alternately, four white, four black, and four red. Commence at A, with the inside row of figures, lift No. 2 over No. 3, No. 2 over No. 1, No. 2 over No. 3, Nos. 2 and 3 over No. 4, and No. 2 over No. 1. Then go to B and change the same way, and so on round table to A. Then go to C, commence with the outside row of figures, and change the same as you did at A, and so on round the table; then you will be through the braid, ready to commence at

A, as at first.

Braid this over a round stick, the size you want the braid for use, varying the number of strands according to the size of the stick; then slip the braid from the stick on to the mold you wish to use, tying it so it will fit the mold exactly, and then boil in water five minutes, and take it out and put it in an oven as hot as it will bear without burning, until it is quite dry. Then it is ready for use.

HALF OPEN BRAID.

TAKE any number of strands that can be divided by four,--sixty being the usual number--fifteen hairs in a strand, and place on table like pattern. Commence at A, with the inside row of figures, lift No. 3 over No. 2, No. 3 over No. 4, No. 1 over No. 2, and No. 3 over No. 2; braid half way round the table, and then braid the last half by lifting No. 3 over No. 2, No. 3 over No. 4, No. 1 over No. 2, No. 3 over No. 2, No. 1 over No. 2, and No. 3 over No. 4, and so on round to A; then go to C and repeat the same. Then you are through the braid, ready to commence as at first.

Braid this over a round stick, the size you want the braid for use, varying the number of strands according to the size of the stick; then slip the braid from the stick on to the mold you wish to use, tying it so it will fit the mold exactly, and then boil in water five minutes, and take it out and put it in an oven as hot as it will bear without burning, until it is quite dry. Then it is ready for use.

OPEN STRIPED BRAID.

TAKE any number of strands that can be divided by four,--eighty being the usual number--four hairs in a strand, and place on table like pattern. Commence at A, with the inside row of figures, and have one-half the strands white hair, and one-half black, and place alternately one strand of white, and one strand of black; lift No. 2 over No. 3, No. 2 over No. 1, No. 2 over No. 3, Nos. 2 and 3 over No. 4, and No. 2 over No. 1. Then go to B and change the same way, and so on round table to A. Then go to C, commence with the outside row of figures, and change the same as at A, and so on round table; then you will be through the braid, ready to commence as at first.

Braid this over a round stick, the size you want the braid for use, varying the number of strands according to the size of the stick; then slip the braid from the stick on to the mold you wish to use, tying it so it will fit the mold exactly, and then boil in water five minutes, and take it out and put it in an oven as hot as it will bear without burning, until it is quite dry. Then it is ready for use.

CHINCHILLA OPEN BRAID.

TAKE any number of strands that can be divided by four,--eighty being the usual number--four hairs in a strand, and place on table like pattern. Commence at A, with the inside row of figures, and have one-half of the strands white hair, and one-half black, and place alternately two strands of white and two of black; lift No. 2 over No. 3, No. 2 over No. 1, No. 2 over No. 3, Nos. 2 and 3 over No. 4, and No. 2 over No. 1; then go to B and change the same way, and so on round table to A. Then go to C, commence with the outside row of figures, and change the same as you did at A, and so on round table. Then you will be through the braid, ready to commence at A, as at first.

Braid this over a round stick, the size you want the braid for use, varying the number of strands according to the size of the stick; then slip the braid from the stick on to the mold you wish to use, tying it so it will fit the mold exactly, and then boil in water five minutes, and take it out and put it in an oven as hot as it will bear without burning, until it is quite dry. Then it is ready for use.

FANCY LACE BRAID.

TAKE any number of strands that can be divided by four,--eighty being the usual number--four hairs in a strand, and place on table like pattern. Commence at A, with the inside row of figures, and have one-half the strands white hair, and one-half black, and place alternately two strands of white, and two strands of black; lift No. 3 over No. 2, No. 3 over No. 4, No. 1 over No.

2, No. 3 over No. 2, No. 1 over No. 2, and No. 3 over No. 4. Then go to B and change the same way, and so on round to A. Then go to C, commence with the outside row of figures, and change the same as you did at A, and so on round table; then you will be through the braid, ready to commence at A, as at first.

Braid this over a round stick, the size you want the braid for use, varying the number of strands according to the size of the stick; then slip the braid from the stick on to the mold you wish to use, tying it so it will fit the mold exactly, and then boil in water five minutes, and take it out and put it in an oven as hot as it will bear without burning, until it is quite dry. Then it is ready for use.

STRIPED ELASTIC BRAID.

TAKE any number of strands that can be divided by four,--sixty being the usual number--fifteen hairs in a strand, and place on table like pattern. Commence at A, with the inside row of figures, and have one-half the strands white hair, and one-half black, and place alternately Nos. 1 and 2 of white, and Nos. 3 and 4 of black; lift No. 1 over No. 2, and No. 4 over Nos. 3 and 2; then repeat with the same strands, the No. 1 over No. 2, and No. 4 over Nos. 3 and 2. Then go to B and braid the same, and so on round table to A. Then go to C, commence with the outside row of figures, and braid round to the left; lift No. 1 over No. 2, and No. 4 over Nos. 3 and 2; then repeat with the same strands, the same as at A and B, and so on round to A. Then you are through the braid, ready to commence as at first. After it is braided, turn the braid inside out.

Braid this over a round stick, the size you want the braid for use, varying the number of strands according to the size of the stick; then slip the braid from the stick on to the mold you wish to use, tying it so it will fit the mold exactly, and then boil in water five minutes, and take it out and put it in an oven as hot as it will bear without burning, until it is quite dry. Then it is ready for use.

OPEN STRIPED BRAID.

TAKE any number of strands that can be divided by four,--sixty being the usual number--fifteen hairs in a strand, and place on table like pattern. Commence at A, with the inside row of figures, and have one-half of the strands white hair, and one-half black, and place alternately one strand of white and one of black; lift No. 1 over No. 2, and No. 4 over Nos. 3 and 2; then repeat with the same strands, the No. 1 over No. 2, and No. 4 over Nos. 3 and 2. Then go to B and braid the same, and so on round table to A. Then go to C, commence with the outside row of figures, and braid round to the left; lift No. 1 over No. 2, and No. 4 over Nos. 3 and 2; then repeat with the same strands, the same as at A and B, and so on round to A. Then you are through the braid, ready to commence as at first. After it is braided, turn the braid inside out.

Braid this over a round stick, the size you want the braid for use, varying the number of strands according to the size of the stick; then slip the braid from the stick on to the mold you wish to use, tying it so it will fit the mold exactly, and then boil in water five minutes, and take it out and put it in an oven as hot as it will bear without burning, until it is quite dry. Then it is ready for use.

WIDE STRIPED BRAID.

TAKE any number of strands that can be divided by four,--eighty being the usual number,--four hairs in a strand, and place on table like pattern. Commence at A, with the inside row of figures, and have one-fourth of the strands white hair, and three-fourths black, and place all the white strands on one side of the table, and all of the black on the other side; lift No. 2 over No. 3, No. 2 over No. 1, No. 2 over No. 3, Nos. 2 and 3 over No. 4, and No. 2 over No. 1. Then go to B and change the same way, and so on round table to A. Then go to C, commence with the outside row of figures, and change the same as at A, and so on round table; then you are through the braid, ready to commence as at first.

Braid this over a round stick, the size you want the braid for use, varying the number of strands according to the size of the stick; then slip the braid from the stick on to the mold you wish to use, tying it so it will fit the mold exactly, and then boil in water five minutes, and take it out and put it in an oven as hot as it will bear without burning, until it is quite dry. Then it is ready for use.

NEAPOLITAN TIGHT BRAID.

TAKE any number of strands that can be divided by four,--eighty being the usual number--four hairs in a strand, and place on table like pattern. Commence at A, with the inside row of figures, and have one-fourth of the strands white hair, and three-fourths black,--the Nos. 1 white, and the Nos. 2, 3 and 4 black; lift No. 3 over No. 2, No. 3 over No. 4, No. 1 over No. 2, and No. 3 over No. 2. Then go to B and change the same way, and so on round table to A. Then go to C, commence with the outside row of figures, and change the same as at A, and so on round table; then you are through the braid, ready to commence as at first.

Braid this over a round stick, the size you want the braid for use, varying the number of strands according to the size of the stick; then slip the braid from the stick on to the mold you wish to use, tying it so it will fit the mold exactly, and then boil in water five minutes, and take it out and put it in an oven as hot as it will bear without burning, until it is quite dry. Then it is ready for use.

OPEN BRAID.

TAKE any number of strands that can be divided by four,--eighty being the usual number for this braid--four hairs in a strand, and place on table like pattern. Commence at A, with the inside row of figures, lift No. 3 over No. 2; then No. 3 over No. 4; then No. 1 over No. 2; then No. 3 over No. 2. Then go to B and change the same way, and so round the table to A. Then go to C, and commence with the outside row of figures, and change the same as you did at A, and so on round the table, when you will be through the braid, ready to commence at A, as at first.

Braid this over a round stick, the size you want the braid for use, varying the number of strands according to the size of the stick; then slip the braid from the stick on to the mold you wish to use, tying the braid so it will fit the mold exactly, and then boil in water five minutes, and take it out and put it in an oven, as hot as it will bear without burning, until it is quite dry. Then it is ready for use.

DIRECTIONS FOR NEW BEGINNERS.

The hair to be used in braiding should be combed perfectly straight, and tied with a string at the roots, to prevent wasting. Then count the number of hairs for a strand, and pull it out from the tips, dip it in water and draw it between the thumb and finger to make it lie smoothly; then tie a solid, single knot at one end, the same as you would with a sewing thread.

THE BOBBIN.

To prepare the bobbin for the hair, wind it with white thread, as shown in the plate, and fasten it with a slip-knot over the knob, leaving an end of some three inches, with a solid knot tied at the end of it. To adjust the hair to the bobbins, take the prepared strands of hair and tie the knotted ends in a square knot to the ends of the strings on the bobbins. When each strand is thus prepared and tied to the bobbin strings, place them even, and tie the ends with a string to prevent their slipping.

See cut of Bobbins on another page.

HOW TO PLACE THEM ON THE TABLE-COVER FOR BRAIDING.

Place the strands across the table-cover, over the numbers, as shown in the diagram, and fasten a weight to the end of them, under the table, through the center of cover; then tie the mold or form to be braided, around in the center, and you are ready for braiding.

For further reference, see plate of table, with explanations.

The Table Cover, as shown in diagram No. 1, represents the under side of the cover, showing the rim that fits over the cap, allowing the cover to revolve, for the convenience of the braider. The cavity through the cover and cap allows the braid, with the weight attached, to pass through as fast as braided.

For reference see Braiding Table complete, with bobbins and weights attached, on page 124.

The above cut represents Braiding Table No. 2, complete, showing the strands over the cover, with Bobbins attached; also, the weight attached to the braid, showing the manner of its passing through the table.

The above cut shows the Wood Bobbins, for fine open work or tight braids. No. 1 is used for braiding any pattern of from one to four hairs in a strand. No. 2 is used for braiding any pattern of from five to twenty hairs in a strand. To prepare the Bobbins for use, see explanations on page 121.

The above cut shows the size and shape of the Lead Bobbins. The No. 1 size is used for braiding Rings and Chains, that have but few hairs in a strand-- from twenty to forty. No. 2 is used for braiding Chains that have from forty to one hundred hairs in a strand. Either size will answer for any pattern of Chain or Ring, but to vary the size of the Bobbin according to the number of hairs in a strand, gives it a nicer finish. To prepare the Bobbin, wind it with thread, as shown in the cut, leaving the thread some three inches long, with a solid knot tied at the end.

The above cut shows the weight used for drawing the work through the center of the table as fast as braided, and to balance the bobbins. Attention should be given to have the weight balance the bobbins properly, as too great a weight will make the braid loose, or too light a weight will leave it rough. Use any number of weights required to balance the bobbins.

The above cuts are made of wire and wood, for braiding over. The Nos. 1 and 2 are for braiding chains over--the No. 1 for small chains, and the No. 2 for large sizes. No. 3 is used for braiding tight or open work braids, of from thirty to forty strands. No. 4 is used for the same braids, with from forty to sixty strands in a braid. The mold may be made any length, to accommodate the work.

The above cuts show the size of forms used for tight or open work braids. The No. 5 is used for braids of from sixty to eighty strands, No. 6 of from eighty to one hundred, and No. 7 from one hundred to one hundred and twenty, according to the fineness of the braid.

The above cuts represent the completed Bracelet Braid. The No. 1 is formed from fourteen small braids, braided according to diagram and explanation on page 104,--using, however, but thirty-two strands, instead of eighty.

After you have the small braids all completed and prepared, as required in the explanation, sew them together at one end, so they all lie smooth and flat, then divide them off in twos, using each two as one strand, and plait them together; commence at the right side, take one strand at a time, and lift over one and under two till you get to the center, then commence on the left side and braid the same way, and so on till finished. Then sew the ends well, trim them, and put on a little shellac to fasten them in the clasps.

No. 2 is from the same pattern, and is prepared and finished up in the same manner. For this Bracelet you use fifteen small braids, divide them into threes for each strand, and lift over one and under one, from each side to the center.

The No. 1 cut of the above Bracelet Braids, is formed from patterns on pages 87 and 97, and instead of using forty and sixty strands, use but thirty-two for each. Braid six small braids from pattern on page 87, and three from pattern on page 97. Sew them tight together at one end, divide them off in threes, with the open work braid between the two tight ones, use each three as one strand, and plait them together in a common three strand braid.

No. 2 is braided according to pattern on page 89. Have three of the braids, sew them fast at one end, and then twist them carefully and evenly together; then sew and fasten with shellac, and it is ready for being gold mounted.

The No. 1 cut of the above Bracelet Braids, is formed from patterns on pages 26 and 86. Have two small braids from each of the patterns, lay them side by side, as in cut, and sew them firmly together, either with some of the hair, or with very fine silk of the same color. Then sew and trim the ends, and fasten with shellac.

No. 2 is braided from patterns on pages 18 and 86. Have four small braids like pattern on page 18, and two like pattern on page 86. Place them side by side, as in cut, and prepare and finish up the same as in the above.

The patterns used for the No. 1, represented above, are found on pages 63 and 95. Have one braid from pattern on page 63, and two from that on page 95. Place them side by side, as in cut, sew the ends firmly together, either with some of the hair, or with very fine silk of the same color. Then sew and trim the ends, and fasten with shellac.

For the No. 2, use two small braids from pattern on page 18, one from pattern on page 63, and two from pattern on page 95. Place them as in cut, sew them together, and prepare the same as No. 1.

The No. 1 of the above Bracelet Braids, is made up of two small braids from pattern on page 97, and three from pattern on page 101, using, however, but thirty-two strands, instead of sixty. Place them side by side, as in cut, and sew them together with some of the hair, or with fine silk of the same color. Sew, trim and shellac the ends, and they are ready for the gold mounting.

No. 2 is formed of four small braids, from pattern on page 97, and is prepared, sewed and finished up the same as No. 1.

LITHOGRAPHED DESIGNS.

The following Lithographic designs of Hair Jewelry, Flowers and Pictures, are given for the purpose of showing a few of the many beautiful forms into which the human hair may be transposed. Each and every one of the devices on the following pages, with the exception of the flowers and pictures, can be braided from the diagrams and explanations given in the first one hundred and twenty pages of this book. Select any article you may wish to make, and by referring to the patterns, you can easily find the style and directions whereby to braid it. We might have given twice the number of patterns, or even more, but any person can, after a little experience, readily invent new and different styles of braids, and by so doing, each can satisfy their own peculiar taste.

The making of Hair Flowers is very simple, and yet, of course, every one has first to learn it. Supply yourself with as many different colors of hair as you can, and by applying Gum Tragacanth, it renders it capable of being cut in any shape you may wish--such as leaves, twigs, buds, &c., and by judiciously arranging the colors, the effect will be very pleasing. Pictures are made in the same manner, and any one possessing the least artistic skill, can make any flower or picture they may desire, and many pleasing adornments and lasting mementos may thereby be had.

All articles intended to be worn as jewelry, should, of course, be mounted with gold, and as this kind of work is not done in all jewelry establishments, I wish to say that my facilities for this branch of business is complete, and the work done is in the best possible manner. I can guarantee satisfaction in all cases, let the style desired be what it may. In sending braids to be mounted, draw on paper, as near as can be, the style or design you want.

[Transcriber's Note: For this text edition, fifty instances of the [Illustration] tag were removed at this point. This was done in an effort to make reading the text less tedious. The actual illustrations can, of course, be seen in the

WEAVING HAIR FOR SWITCHES.

The above cut represents the apparatus used for weaving hair into Switches, Curls, Wigs, &c. It is a very simple arrangement, and can be easily constructed. Provide two straight sticks, about twelve inches long, and in one of them bore three small holes, two inches apart, in which to place as many thumb-screws, to be used for tightening or loosening the cords; in the other, have a single wooden pin or nail, to fasten the cords to. Place the sticks in a firm, upright position, about three feet apart, either by boring holes through a table, or by using mortised blocks, such as is plainly shown in cut, at the right end. After placing them in position, put on three cords, as shown in diagram, numbered 1, 2 and 3. For this weft use linen thread, at Nos. 1, 2 and 3.

In commencing to weave, place the hair between two cards, as shown in diagram, and draw out with the right hand, between the thumb and fore-finger, the quantity of hair required for the size of the weft; then change it into the left hand, and place it up to the threads, Nos. 1, 2 and 3, as shown in diagram; lay the strand over No. 1, under No. 2, over No. 3, around under No. 3, over Nos. 2 and 1, around under Nos. 1 and 2, over No. 3, around under Nos. 3 and 2, and over No. 1. Then push the strands together, as in cut.

The No. 1 of the above cuts represents the winding and sewing of the switch after it is woven. For sewing a switch on points, after weaving, take Berlin cord, about one-sixteenth of an inch thick, and tie a solid knot at the end, and sew the end of the weft to the knotted end of the cord; then wind the weft around the cord, as shown in cut, the length of point desired, turning the end of the cord over to form a loop. Cut the weft according to the number of points desired in the switch. Cut No. 2 shows the switch all complete.

WEAVING HAIR FOR CURLS.

In commencing to weave, place the hair between two cards, or stiff brushes, as shown in diagram, pressing them tight together, so that in drawing out, it is perfectly free from tangles; draw out with the right hand, between the thumb and fore-finger, the quantity of hair required for the size of the weft; then change it into the left hand, and lift it up to the No. 1 cord, as shown in diagram; lay the strand over No. 1, under No. 2, over No. 3, around under No. 3, over Nos. 2 and 1, around under Nos. 1 and 2, over No. 3, around under No. 3, over No. 2, and under No. 1. Then push the strands together, as shown in diagram. For this weft use fine, strong linen thread.

MAKING AND PREPARING CURLS.

After weaving, according to directions on page 241, take a piece of ribbon an inch wide, the same color of hair, and as long as you wish the curls to be in width, and sew the weft to it back and forth. After that is done, pipe them, which is done in this manner: Dampen the hair, comb each curl out straight, and wind it tightly on a rattan stick about four inches long, having each curl on a separate stick, and commencing to wind at the tip end, tying them firmly to keep in place. Then boil in water for thirty minutes, and place in an oven as hot as they will bear without burning, until quite dry. When dry and perfectly cool, take them off the sticks, and smooth over a curling iron, the size you wish the curls. Side curls and frizzes should be prepared the same way.

Cut No. 2 represents a set of Curls and Puffs. For explanation of Puffs, see page 245.

WEAVING HAIR FOR WIGS.

In commencing to weave, place the hair between two cards, or stiff brushes, as shown in diagram, pressing them tight together, so that in drawing out, it is perfectly free from tangles; draw out with the right hand, between the thumb and fore-finger, the quantity of hair required for the size of the weft; then change it into the left hand, and lift it up to the No. 1 cord, as shown in diagram; lay the strand over No. 1, under No. 2, over No. 3, around under No.

3, over Nos. 2 and 1, around under Nos. 1 and 2, over No. 3, around under No. 3, over Nos. 2 and 1, around under Nos. 1 and 2, over No. 3 around under Nos. 3 and 2, and over No. 1. Then push the strands together, as shown in diagram. For this weft use sewing silk.

WEAVING HAIR FOR WATERFALLS AND BOWS

Prepare the same as above, and place the strand under No. 1, over Nos. 2 and 3, around under Nos. 3 and 2, over No. 1, around under Nos. 1 and 2, over No. 3, around under No. 3, and over Nos. 2 and 1. Aside from these changes, follow directions given above.

MAKING WATERFALLS AND BOWS.

In making a Chignon, you have first to make the cushion. Take the combings or waste hair, which is of no other use, and place it between the cards or stiff brushes, the same as for weaving. Use the weaving apparatus, with two piping cords, instead of three small ones, and wind the hair all up, by passing over, between and under the cords. Boil and dry it, and then pull out the cord, which leaves it all crimped, ready to weave, according to directions on page 239. Then sew it on a cord, the same as a switch, and form it in any shape you desire, for a Waterfall, Bow or Puffs. This completes the cushion. Then weave the long hair for the covering, according to directions on page 243, and sew it to the top end of the cushion; comb it out smooth, cover the cushion, and tie a cord around it immediately at the bottom; then bring up the end of the hair, and pin it to the inside. Cut No. 1 is intended to represent the cushion, and No. 2 the complete Waterfall.

Cut No. 3 represents the Bow, which is made in the same manner, by using two small cushions, like cut No. 1, and placing between them a strand of smooth or braided hair.

MAKING PUFFS AND COILS.

To make Puffs for front of head, from false hair, similar to cut No. 1, weave hair from eight to twelve inches long, according to directions on page 241; then take a ribbon, about one and a half inches wide, any length required, and tack it on a wig block, or straight piece of board, and sew the weft crossways a quarter of an inch apart, till the ribbon is entirely covered; then divide it off in as many puffs as desired, comb each out straight, and wind it over the two fore-fingers, close up to ribbon, and put in a hair-pin to retain it.

To make Puffs for back of head, cut No. 2, prepare the same way; make the foundation the shape and size you wish the puffs, and sew it on the same way you want the puffs to run. The puffs may be made over a cushion, formed of crimped hair the shape wanted, and wound over that instead of the fingers. Ladies not wearing false hair, can have her own hair dressed by following the above directions.

Cut No. 3 represents a coil, which is made from a switch, and wound over a long roll of crimped hair. They are much nicer, but more expensive, by being made altogether from a switch, as that can be twisted into a rope or braided, before coiling.

EXPLANATIONS ON HAIR DRESSING.

I herewith present, on the following pages, a number of engravings illustrative of a few of the many styles of Hair Dressing, accompanied with explanatory remarks as to their execution. They are the latest and most fashionable European and American styles, and will prove indispensable to every lady's toilet, as, from the explanations, they will be able, with very little practice, to dress their own hair in any desired style; and when any new style is inaugurated, after studying and practicing the directions given with each illustration, she will find it an easy matter to arrange it accordingly.

Any one learning Hair Dressing, should acquire perfectly the execution of the first pattern--the Promenade Head-Dress--as that is very easily arranged, and when you have once executed it in a perfect manner, the others will prove comparatively easy.

The manner of dressing the hair at the present day calls for much attention, and many inquiries are addressed us on the subject. It is plain, however, that what would correspond with the complexion and physiognomy of one, would certainly have a distasteful appearance on another; consequently, in answering inquiries, I can do nothing more than give the different styles worn. Before giving my illustrations on Hair Dressing, I have given instructions how to weave hair for chignons, curls, switches, &c., and how to put them in shape, and with the directions given with each illustration on Hair Dressing, it will certainly be an easy task to arrange the hair in any style that is now or may be in fashion.

Our first cut represents the Promenade Head-Dress, but is worn as frequently in the drawing-room, and even at public and private assemblies--in fact, a common and very pretty style.

EXPLANATION: Comb the front hair between the temples straight back, over a cushion of crimped hair, forming a Chignon; then make two braids of two small switches, and place one of them over the top of the Chignon, and the other across the forehead, forming a diadem, turning the ends under; then comb the hair from temples over the braids, and put back under the Chignon, and fasten. Place a net of pearl or gilt beads over the Chignon, as in cut. You can use false hair for covering cushion, if desired.

This Head-Dress is a most charming composition, and entirely new. It is adapted either for a brown or fair complexion, to be worn at grand dinners or receptions. Ornamented with pearl or gilt, it is in good taste for evening parties.

EXPLANATION: Curl the hair across forehead, or use false curls, combing the hair straight back, and form a chignon of curls at the back. Place a diadem plait across forehead, and raise the hair from the temples over the plait. Trim with roses and ribbans, or to suit dress.

This cut illustrates the Soiree or Evening Head-Dress. It is a very unique and modern style, suited for almost any complexion, and very easily executed.

EXPLANATION: Comb the hair straight back between the temples, tie it, and curl the ends, or use a set of long false curls. Place a diadem plait, made from a switch, across the forehead; then comb the hair back from the temples, over the ends of the plait, twist it, pass it back under the curls, and fasten firmly. Use a fancy back-comb on top of curls, and pin an ornament to diadem plait, with feather and chain attached, as in cut, or trim to suit dress.

A very graceful Head-Dress, of a bold style, suited for a young lady of brown or fair complexion, and is in good taste to be worn at the theatre or Grand Evening Parties.

EXPLANATION: Make a parting over the head, from ear to ear, two inches from front; on the forehead, between the temples, curl the hair in small friz curls, and from the temple to the ear, make loose puffs. Divide the hair in three partings over the head, and roll each in a large puff; then form a large puff of the back hair, round the nape of the neck, as in cut. Fasten a large set of loose curls over the puff, with a comb or other ornament. For reference, see page 245.

A charming Head-Dress, and entirely new, perfectly suiting a fair complexion. It may serve for the theatre or evening parties. When powdered it preferably suits a brown or brunette.

EXPLANATION: Make a front parting, and a cross one from ear to ear. Divide each side into five parts; of the front parting make three puffs on each side. The remaining four make into long puffs, as in cut, according to explanations on page 245. The back hair may be arranged in the same style of puffs, or with a double Chignon, placing a single, long false curl or braid, back of each ear. Trim with orange leaves, or to suit dress.

This Head-Dress, both bold and graceful, is suitable for any complexion or age, when the physiognomy allows it.

EXPLANATION: Comb back the hair from the forehead between the temples, make a large puff on the temples, and three puffs above each ear. Place a cushion at the back of head, and comb the hair over it, forming a chignon; then place a diadem plait, or twist, made from a large switch, round on the top of head, trimmed with leaves or ribbon, as shown in cut.

This Head-Dress is one of the most graceful styles. It was worn in the time of Louis XIVth, and well agrees with the fashion of the present day. With some modifications, it is suited to every complexion.

EXPLANATION: Crimp the front hair, and raise it over the temples with a puff comb. Comb the hair just above the ear back, and friz the ends, and curl the back hair in large flowing curls, as shown in the cut.

A Head-Dress of elegant composition, coming down from antiquity, suitable for a young and pretty woman, and perfectly agreeing with a fair complexion.

EXPLANATION: Part the hair from temple to temple, one inch from front, comb it up on the forehead, and curl the ends in small snap curls; then comb the hair back from the temples, and form a loose puff. Make three partings across the head, and form a puff of each. Of the back hair, make a braided or plaited chignon, with a few friz curls underneath; then make two puffs back of the ear, as shown in cut. Wear a fancy comb or band over the top of chignon.

A Head-Dress of extraordinary simplicity, and of a most genteel kind, becoming a dark complexion. It may be adapted for the opera by changing the trimming.

EXPLANATION: First crimp all the hair, then place a cushion high up under the hair at the back, forming a chignon, and friz the ends of the hair from ear to ear under the chignon. Tuck the hair high up on the forehead, place bands of ribbon over the head with a net at the back, and bring the hair above the ear up, and fasten to the ribbon. Pin a ribbon streamer to the net, as in cut.

An elegant Head-Dress, and was worn in the time of Louis XVI, for balls and evening parties, or as a disguise when powdered.

EXPLANATION: Separate the hair across the head from ear to ear, three inches from front, and roll it in puffs according to directions on page 245. Do up the back hair in a double chignon, either with your own or false hair; add a set of false curls underneath the chignon, extending from ear to ear. Trim to suit dress with leaves, flowers and ribbon, as shown in illustration.

A rich Head-Dress, having a great stamp of distinction, and for that reason will be adapted for a Court Head-Dress, or Grand Evening Parties.

EXPLANATION: Make a parting over the head from ear to ear, two inches from front, and form a row of nine small puffs over the forehead. Comb the remaining hair back, and divide into four partings around the head, and form each parting in a large puff, as in cut. Add a few small friz curls and orange blossoms between the puffs. For reference see page 245.

An exquisite Head-Dress, of a very graceful style, and well agreeing with a fair or brown complexion, to be worn by a young bride, or at grand assemblies.

EXPLANATION: Comb the hair back and place a set of small loose curls across the forehead; place a diadem plait over the top of the curls, and comb the hair off the temples over the ends of the plait, and form a chignon or bow of the back hair, and place a three-strand braid around the chignon, made either from the ends of hair from the temple or a switch. Add a crown of white blossoms and a veil, as shown in the engraving. If not for a bride, trim to match dress.

An exquisite Head-Dress, of exceedingly graceful and modern style, agreeing with nearly every complexion; may be worn as a promenade or at small parties.

EXPLANATION: Part the hair from front to crown, and from ear to ear; crimp the front, and braid the ends in a three-strand braid, and trim the ends with ribbon. Either braid or twist the back hair, and form into a coil. Place a small plait across the forehead, as shown in the engraving. Deck the hair with flowers or beads, to suit the occasion.

SYNOPTIC OF HUMAN HAIR.

In placing before the public the only book ever published in the "Art of Hair Work," it is but due to the purchasers of it to say something in relation to the trade in Human Hair. It is not my intention, however, to enter into an extended detail and complete history, but simply give a few items that will serve to show what enormous strides have been taken within the last few years in this branch of business. It is a business that but few know anything about--at least in this country, for it is comparatively new here--but it is one that is very rapidly increasing, and is now almost doubling itself each year.

The larger quantity, in fact nearly the whole amount of hair retailed in this country is imported from Europe, where the dealing in human hair has been made an established and legitimate business for years, and a great deal of attention is paid in purchasing and preparing it for the market. Paris is the greatest market for the sale of human hair in the world; but the amount of superfluous hair used and worn throughout all Europe, could we give the figures, would seem incredible. The amount imported to the United States in the years of 1859 and 1860 was not far from 150,000 and 200,000 pounds, which was valued at that time at from $800,000 to $1,000,000. Since that time it has been steadily increasing, and the amount imported last year may be set down at three times as much as during the years above mentioned. Paris also finds as great a sale for the article in Russia as in America--the shipments to each being about equal. Thus, it will be seen, that if all the hair reserved in Europe for the home demand were added to that which is imported, the amount would be almost beyond conception; and yet, but about one-tenth part of the whole production ever leaves its native country.

It is mostly procured from the markets of France, Italy, Russia and Germany, and large quantities are obtained from Norway and Sweden.

The Norwegians were among the first to make ornaments of hair to be worn as jewelry, but, in a great measure, we are indebted to the French for the perfection to which the art has attained. Of the different varieties of hair, that which is obtained in France and Italy is by far the best, being of a much finer texture, even color, and of a more glossy appearance than that from other countries.

The principal requirement in hair to make it valuable is length, and after it is thrown upon the market it is all assorted--the long from the short--which is a task of extreme difficulty.

The prices of hair range all the way from $15 to $200 per pound, (a wide range, but certainly not too large,) and is rated according to hue, length and texture. The smallest price paid is for the short, coarse hair of the poorest quality, and which can be used only for certain purposes. Hair of the ordinary colors range in price from $15 to $100 per pound, but that of gray and white from $100 to $200 per pound, and even then is not considered exorbitant. In fact, hair is worth any and all prices. We know of one dealer who had in his possession a very small quantity, weighing but a half pound and measuring seventy inches, for which he was offered four hundred dollars! and, strange as it may appear, he refused to accept it. White hair is mostly obtained by being picked from the gray, and it not unfrequently happens that many hundred pounds have to be assorted before being able to secure one single pound of pure white. It is mainly used in the manufacture of wigs, and it frequently puzzles the dealer to prepare one for a customer that will exactly match, and this, with the scarcity of the article, cause the extraordinary price.

Hair is shipped in both a prepared and unprepared state. That which is prepared undergoes a process of washing, scouring and cleansing, which leaves it in the nicest possible state; all the oil, dirt and other unhealthy substances are completely separated from it, leaving it perfectly free from all unhealthy influences. That which is shipped in an unprepared, or raw state, is subjected to the same process of cleansing after its arrival, and it is so thorough that it is altogether impossible for anything except the hair to remain. It has frequently been examined with a microscope, which has proved in every case how successful the cleansing process had been, for it revealed nothing whatever of a foreign nature, and, in fact, after its extraordinary cleaning it would be simply impossible.

After being fully prepared it is then made into switches, curls, plaits, fronts, wigs, chignons, and not a small amount is used in the manufacture of hair jewelry, and such other articles as are worn for ornaments. The jewelry manufactured at this time is as durable as the all gold jewelry, and is done in a style of surpassing neatness, thus rendering it beautiful, either as an ornament or memento. There are but very few places in the United States where hair jewelry is made, and as it is comparatively a new business, but few have learned it. It is surprising, however, to notice the many beautiful patterns and elegant designs into which it is transformed. There is nothing in the way of jewelry or ornament of any description but what is or may be made from human hair; and, after being gold-mounted, the contrast between them makes the hair jewelry preferable to the all gold.

There are many strange incidents related of the human hair suddenly changing its color--many of which it is hard to believe--and the causes assigned are various. We are told of persons who, from excessive grief, found their hair had gradually changed from a dark brown to an almost perfect white; others, from the same cause, in the short space of one week discovered their hair plentifully streaked with grey, giving them the appearance, although young, of being quite old. Many have had their hair change on account of extreme fright, but we have now to give the first instance we have ever heard of its turning from white to that of any other color, except by the aid of dyes.

A Parisian, M. Stanislaus Martin, has published in the Bulletin de Therapeutique the curious case of a worker in metals who had wrought in copper only five months, and whose hair, which was lately white, is now of so decided a green that the man cannot appear in the street without immediately becoming the object of general curiosity. He is perfectly well, his hair alone being affected by the copper, notwithstanding the precautions taken by him to protect it from the action of the metal. Chemical analysis shows that his hair contains a notable quantity of acetate of copper, and that it is to this circumstance that it owes its beautiful green color, which is most singular and remarkable.

The practice of wearing false hair, although it was not generally dealt in as traffic, has been in vogue many hundred years. The Greek and Roman ladies were, in olden times, as active in their toilet for the head as the fashionable ladies of the present day, and false hair was always brought into requisition, which was then obtained from the Germans, and they in turn from their slaves.

Powdering the hair, which is now the rage in all fashionable circles, is also an ancient practice, and was as much indulged in by the men as the women. History tells us that the consumption of hair powder by the soldiers of George II was enormous. It was calculated, that inasmuch as the military force of England and the colonies was, including cavalry, infantry, militia and fensibles, 250,000, each man used a pound of flour a week, simply for powdering their hair. The quantity consumed in this way was 6,500 tons per annum; an amount sufficient to sustain 30,000 persons on bread. Gold and silver hair powder was also plentifully used, and at a time much earlier in the world's history, than is generally supposed. Josephus relates that Solomon's horse-guards daily strewed their heads with gold-dust, which glittered in the sun; and there are similar instances of different personages recorded in the bible.

The human hair seems to have been given us both for an ornament and covering--being susceptible of transformation in almost any desired shape, and apparently indispensable for covering and protecting the head. The ancient Greeks were very partial to long hair, considering it by far the more becoming; but the Egyptians regarded it as an incumbrance, shaved their heads, and substituted wigs. The ancients, generally speaking, strangely considered a fine head of hair so desirable, that it became sacred. They frequently dedicated it to the gods, on important occasions of marriage, victory, escape from death and danger, and the burial of friends. Different styles of wearing the hair, was resorted to for denoting the various grades, or positions in life, of the people, some wearing it quite long, others short, and some dressing it in a peculiar manner,--each style, or length, being according to the condition, wealth, or social standing of the wearer. Plucking it out, or neglecting it, was a token of affliction.

Hair contains a very small quantity of water, manganese, iron, and various salts of lime, which have been found by the various methods of analyzation, and it is owing to these properties that it is peculiarly indestructible. It has been found on mummies, more than twenty centuries old, in a perfect and unaltered state, and many instances are related, which are now admitted to be facts, of the hair continuing to grow, for a time, after death.

There has never before been a book written and published, that was particularly dedicated to the subject of Hair, and as the field is a vast one, both as regards the importance of the subject, and the information to be gained thereby, it is simply strange that no one has ever entered it. It has been too long neglected, and the increasing necessity for a treatise of this kind, has been pressed upon the attention of the author, and induced the publication of this work, which will certainly meet the necessities of the age.

There is much else that might be said on this subject that would prove both interesting and instructive, but we prefer for the present to let it rest. We have endeavored in preparing this book both to instruct and amuse; for, by following its instructions, it may be made to be profitable and highly remunerative, and in making articles, either for gifts, mementoes, or otherwise, it will certainly be amusing and entertaining. We have given the instructions in a way that all may readily understand, and as the patterns are numerous, and the designs elegant, we think there can be nothing lacking to make the book all it claims to be.

###

www.ingramcontent.com/pod-product-compliance
Lightning Source LLC
Chambersburg PA
CBHW062016280526
45787CB00005B/2125